THE CASE AGAINST

THE CASE AGAINST

P. J. HOLT

sussex
ACADEMIC
PRESS
Brighton • Chicago • Toronto

2 4 6 8 10 9 7 5 3 1

First published in 2019 in Great Britain by
SUSSEX ACADEMIC PRESS
PO Box 139
Eastbourne BN24 9BP

Distributed in North America by
SUSSEX ACADEMIC PRESS
Independent Publishers Group
814 N. Franklin Street
Chicago, IL 60610

British Library Cataloguing in Publication Data
A CIP catalogue record for this book is available from the British Library.

Library of Congress Cataloging-in-Publication Data
Names: Holt, P. J., author.
Title: God : the case against / P.J. Holt.
Description: Chicago : Sussex Academic Press, 2019. |
Includes index.
Identifiers: LCCN 2018047899 | ISBN 9781845199685
   (pbk : alk. paper)
Subjects: LCSH: God. | God—Proof. | Atheism.
Classification: LCC BL473 .H65 2019 | DDC 212—dc23
LC record available at https://lccn.loc.gov/2018047899

	MIX
®	**MIX**
FSC www.fsc.org	Paper from responsible sources **FSC® C013056**

Typeset & designed by Sussex Academic Press, Brighton & Eastbourne.
Printed by TJ International, Padstow, Cornwall.

CONTENTS

PREFACE

This book is about something of supreme importance to all of us. That is, whether there is a God and a life after death for us human beings. It is an old question, and you are bound to have already thought about it – in fact you probably already have your own 'answers', even if these are vague and uncertain. But unless you are a philosopher or theologian (and this book is not intended for them!) you probably have not examined the questions in a clear, systematic way, free from prejudice and *unaffected by views instilled in childhood* when you were unable to assess them properly. This book, written for ordinary people and not philosophical experts, attempts to put that right.

You need no prior knowledge to read this book, just an enquiring and open mind and reasonable intelligence. There are none of those irritating references to other books that you haven't read. The aim throughout is clarity and, wherever possible, simplicity. It has to be admitted that some of the discussions in the book require effort and perhaps reflection over a period of time – philosophy is like that, it can't be helped. But no *technical* knowledge is needed. You can't do higher mathematics or nuclear physics without massive and very difficult background knowledge.But any intelligent person can understand and reflect on this material and is as likely to get things right as a philosopher or theologian!

I myself am an experienced teacher of mathematics

and physics as well as philosophy. I believe I can therefore combine the scientific and philosophical approaches to problems, which can sometimes be in conflict. I am a trained philosopher (winner of the C.E.M. Joad prize) and an author of five mathematics textbooks as well as some philosophical work. This has given me a strong awareness of the importance of clarity and simplicity in explanatory writing.

There is no hostility to religion in the book: the stance taken is that the 'God' theory is an attempt to deal with genuine problems which in fact fails but which can be viewed sympathetically. I myself had a religious upbringing which I look on with gratitude and affection.

The approach is individual, owing nothing to other authors. I believe that the case for God's existence is *significantly weaker than generally realised*. I try to demonstrate this, and I also examine the *concepts and language* we use in speaking of God and the 'supernatural'. These can lead to error because they are necessarily based on our lives in this material world and do not easily 'transfer' to an entirely different realm. This is not always evident to unreflecting religious believers.

The final chapter examines the principal alternative to the God theory, which is materialism. This also is shown to present difficulties. The conclusion is that *informed puzzlement* may be the appropriate, unavoidable final position. The idea of God may not solve the problems it is usually believed to solve (such as the origin of the universe, and the moral law) but dispensing with God does not mean that those problems disappear. The universe and we human beings who inhabit it still throw up mysteries and puzzles which we are as yet unable to solve.

A small preliminary point: Throughout this book I will adopt the usual practice of referring to God as 'he'. I hope this will not annoy readers. Obviously God can be neither male nor female, but the practice is so long-established that any other pronoun now sounds unnatural.

CHAPTER ONE
THE PROBLEM

Is there a God? Is there a life after death? Does it matter how we behave in this life? Will God (if he exists) judge us when we die and reward or punish us?

These questions matter to all of us, and I suppose that just about every adult person, if questioned, would come out with some sort of opinion on each of them – even if only, 'It's impossible to tell.' Of course, there is a good deal of variation in how much and how deeply the questions are considered: probably most people nowadays just get on with their lives and worry about deeper matters only when something unusual happens, such as the death of a loved one or a serious illness. Still, this kind of event does happen to a majority of us eventually, and must surely provoke some kind of reflection on our questions. So I think it is fair to say that all normal human beings will hold some opinions about these matters, even if such views are vague and imprecise.

There are essentially three distinguishable responses to our questions, corresponding to three kinds of belief. The first is technically known as *theism*, and it means belief in God. This will normally be accompanied by the belief that we human beings will have a life after death. The second is *atheism*, which is the direct opposite. There is no God and no life after death. The third is *agnosticism*, which is usually taken to mean simply that the person concerned cannot decide. I think it is more useful, however, to define agnosticism as the view that the arguments and evidence *do not justify* any definite belief either way. The difference is perhaps slight, but the second definition implies that the question has been fully investigated before a decision is reached. I want the description 'agnostic' to mean more than just a person who has not bothered to think about the matter.

A word is perhaps needed about the term 'God'. Should I throw it in so casually as if its meaning is perfectly straightforward and unproblematic, when the concept is so complex and God himself, if he exists, almost certainly beyond our full understanding? Well, at this stage I want to keep things as simple as possible, so let us just say that I am using the traditional idea of God as a supreme, unique being, morally perfect, with unlimited knowledge and power, who is the designer and creator of our universe. He is normally supposed to have laid down moral rules for us, and he judges us according to how we have kept those rules during our natural lives. After which he rewards or punishes us – with perfect justice, of course – in an afterlife.

The above questions have already, of course, been discussed by philosophers and theologians *ad nauseam*. Since there is certainly no general agreement about the answers, I think it is fair to say that nothing remotely like a *proof* has ever been found, or is likely to be found, either of the existence or non-existence of God. Genuine proofs, by definition, are accepted by all people capable of understanding the terms and reasoning used. Nobody disputes the proof of Pythagoras's Theorem. For myself, I find that if I run through any attempt at a proof – say of the existence of God – I immediately become convinced of its inadequacy. But if I then try adopting – tentatively and experimentally, so to speak – the opposite position, I find that there are still difficulties, things that cause puzzlement. If, for example, I consider materialism – the usual alternative to belief in God – I react rapidly with the conviction that this also has unsatisfactory features. There are facts about ourselves and the universe which the theory does not fully explain. We shall look at some of these in the final chapter.

So is agnosticism the only rationally justifiable position? Well, possibly. But I don't think one should jump too readily to that 'solution' – it has too much of an air of giving up the struggle. It may be that agnosticism is, ultimately, unavoidable – after all, I have already pointed out that all attempts at proofs have failed – but I feel that it should be a last resort – we should at least have a look at the difficulties that arise with the two main positions. The hope is that this will be interesting and instructive.

In this book I want to avoid anything *technical* – anything requiring specialised knowledge of the kind that philosophers and theologians are supposed to have. I intend to look at the reasons why *ordinary people* so often believe in God, and consider whether these are adequate. It may of course be said, cynically, that most people believe in God because they are brought up to do so, and they become used to their religious beliefs and practices and never really question them. This no doubt is so in many cases. But I suspect that few religious believers would admit this if asked to defend their position. They would claim that their beliefs are rationally based. So let us start by asking what reasons they would give.

There seem to be two main lines of thought. The

first concerns the universe – the material universe in which we live. Both its very existence and the laws it obeys seem to demand an explanation. In particular the physical laws are striking in their permanence and regularity. They operate, and presumably always have operated, unchangingly over the whole enormous extent of the universe for an unimaginably vast length of time. They enable us to lead our normal, regular lives, planning ahead with absolute confidence that the physical world will behave in the future just as it has in the past. This structured, regular, law-governed universe can even seem to have the mysterious quality *beauty* to many people. Now surely such a universe, in which intelligent beings such as ourselves can live regular, often fulfilling lives, must have been deliberately designed. I have heard this line of thinking – often expressed in a hesitant, inarticulate way – many times. 'The earth and the stars didn't make themselves, did they?' Whether or not this reasoning is valid, it certainly has real persuasive power for most religious believers. Our beautiful, structured universe requires a designer. And the only being we have heard of who could possibly satisfy this demand is of course God. He is supposed to have the power both to design the universe and create it.

The second line of reasoning uses *moral* considerations – ideas about right and wrong, good and evil. Briefly, this world does not satisfy our ordinary ideas of moral *justice*. Too often good people suffer, while evil, wicked ones do well, or at least are not adequately punished. Surely, we feel, this cannot really be the way the universe is set up; Stalin and Hitler *must*, eventually, pay for their cruelty and Mother Teresa (say) will be rewarded for the good she has done. The usual 'remedy' for the injustice of this life is to suppose that things will be 'put right' in a life after death. This of course requires an all-wise, powerful and perfectly good God to make the correct moral judgements and implement them.

The usual alternative to a belief in God is what might be called the *universe as brute fact* theory. A 'brute' fact is a basic fact, one which might be used to explain other facts, but which cannot be explained itself. When confronted with a brute fact we can only respond with: that is just the way things are; there is nothing more to be said. It seems on the face of it that there must be brute facts, for explanation must end somewhere. We might explain fact A by reference to fact B, then fact B in terms of fact C, and so on; but eventually this sequence must surely stop: there must, it seems, be facts which are simply true and that is all.

If this line of thinking is accepted, the key question is where our brute facts are to be located. A theist will naturally claim that God is the one entity which explains all else. The universe, and anything else which may exist, is created by God: he himself is the single non-created being and there can be no explanation of his own existence: if there were it would imply some-thing 'prior', so to speak, to God, and he would not be the single being from which all else derives.

But suppose we reject the God hypothesis. We think the arguments for his existence are invalid, or at least inadequate – probably we are suspicious of any 'supernatural' explanations for the phenomena we observe. Well the obvious position to take then is that the universe itself is just brute fact. Why should that be less satisfactory than the God view? Remember that brute facts cannot, by definition, be explained, so it seems on the face of it that no brute fact can be more probable, plausible, satisfactory, than any other.

And we are at least quite certain that the universe exists, while the existence of God can surely be no more than a theory.

It must be admitted that this 'solution' leaves the moral problem (the second main argument in favour of God) apparently unsolved; but the typical atheist is usually willing to live with this. He or she will probably say that moral considerations are a function of human behaviour and it is up to us, human beings, to put things right when our (flawed) human nature leads to suffering and injustice. There is no other remedy and we just have to accept that.

I will say now that I do not myself find the 'universe as brute fact' theory appealing or convincing. It is hard to believe that such a complex, ordered universe simply exists, with no explanation. But that does not, in itself, force us to adopt the God theory. It may be that feelings of what is plausible are no guide to the truth; human knowledge and understanding are, after all, very limited. Perhaps there is some third theory, or it may simply be that the truth is beyond human understanding. My main intention now is to examine the God hypothesis. This is still accepted by billions of people throughout the world and affects the lives of those billions. I myself believe that it does not stand up to analysis – indeed the God theory does not even, in my opinion, provide a valid solution to the problems outlined above which the theory is supposed to solve. (That is the apparent need for an explanation of the universe and the conviction we feel that our moral behaviour matters and demands reward or punishment.) But whether it is right or wrong, in view of the vast number of people who accept the existence of God, the truth or falsity of that view is of unquestionable importance.

One point should perhaps be made concerning the prevalence of the God theory. We should not make the mistake of thinking that a huge quantity of adherents means that a doctrine must be true, or is more likely to be true. Human error is all too common; we have only to look at past beliefs to see that. Who now believes in witches, evil spirits, even guardian angels? Yet at one time their existence was no doubt generally accepted. Numbers of believers prove nothing. If one ordinary person likes some cheap, sensational, poor quality tabloid newspaper, there will probably be millions of others who enjoy the same paper, simply because there are millions of ordinary people! Numbers are no guide either to quality or the validity of a belief.

Before examining the theory in detail I want to draw the readers' attention to some odd features of the God hypothesis – paradoxes, so to speak, which ought by themselves to give some uneasiness to believers. Most of these are well-known, but, perhaps because they are familiar, they are usually ignored, or tolerated, or treated as above human understanding. (This last is a very common 'move', in theological debate.) Let us look at a few of them.

I will take first the 'problem of suffering'. This is a very old, well-known objection to God (or source of puzzlement about God): there is a long exposition in the *Book of Job*, in the Old Testament. But it should not be supposed that just because the problem is old, it must have been solved. It has not – at any rate in a way that would generally be regarded as acceptable. The problem of suffering (along with the closely related 'problem of evil') has always been, and remains, one of the most powerful objections to the God theory.

Curiously, the existence of suffering and injustice on this earth was given above as a reason for *belief* in God:

we said that the unfairness of this world could only be 'put right' in an afterlife in which God rewards or punishes us. But this actually ignored a more fundamental problem, which is to explain why an all-powerful and morally perfect creator should allow such suffering in the first place! And the whole history of mankind is a catalogue of appalling suffering. We have plagues, such as the Black Death, famine, massacres, agonising diseases like cancer, and a depressing sequence of wars, which are always a cause of immense pain and injustice. In fact, for most of mankind the interludes of pleasure and/or happiness have been all too infrequent and brief. Yet God, if he exists, knew in advance that this would happen and still chose to create ourselves and our universe.

There have been various attempts at answers, of course, and some seem to 'work' for some cases. For example, human free will, in itself presumably a good thing, is a cause of some suffering since human beings can and do choose to do evil. But this does not explain 'natural' calamities, or appallingly painful diseases. Again, it might be claimed that suffering can be beneficial to some humans. They may profit spiritually from the 'struggle', perhaps the noble endurance – after all it is a common belief (if difficult to explain) that a life of pure pleasure is unworthy of human nature. But this does not apply to animal suffering (often ignored, in theological debate), or that of young children or those without the 'spiritual strength' to benefit from suffering. Furthermore a disease like Alzheimer's actually seems to destroy the personality – change the very nature of a person, often to the great distress of relatives. It is hard to see any spiritual benefit here.

As to things being 'put right' in an afterlife, well, do we think this applies to animals? Or perhaps even to

Neanderthal Man? In any case the whole idea of 'cancelling', 'negating', as it were, something bad by something good later on, is highly suspect, as we shall try to show shortly. The usual response to the problem by convinced religious believers is essentially similar to the final conclusion of Job himself. 'Who are we to question God?' 'His ways are not our ways.' 'He is unimaginably far above human understanding.' Etc., etc. This all very well if we are convinced, on other grounds, that God exists. But if God's existence is the question at issue, then behaviour on the part of God which seems to conflict with our idea of an infinitely good and powerful being must tell against this belief.

It is also puzzling why God seems to leave so many of us 'in the dark' about his existence. He is supposed to love us and really care about our welfare and behaviour. And (we are told) he expects us in return to love and worship him, pray to him regularly, thanking him, acknowledging our dependence on him, and so on.

But many people, perfectly sincerely, having considered all the arguments, are simply unable to believe in his existence. Is God being 'fair' to let them be so deluded? And what about all those (for example savages, cannibals) who have had little or no religious education? Or, like the Greeks and Romans, are brought up to believe in many 'gods' (Venus, Mars, Zeus, and so on) rather than the 'one true God'? If we are Christians, and think that Jesus Christ came into the world to enlighten us, well what about all those who lived before Christ? Or who did not happen to hear about him and his teaching? Why are all these people denied knowledge of something so vital? It seems both unfair and counter-productive, if God really made us to 'know him, love him and serve him'.

There is also a good deal of questionable logic in prayer itself. It is understandable that God should want us to acknowledge his existence and our dependence on him, and possibly to ask him for help, particularly help with the difficult task of avoiding sin. But where is the logic in 'thanking' God? Gratitude is something that has grown up and has its 'natural home' in human behaviour, where helping others is often difficult and may require self-sacrifice. But God can do all things with no effort at all, and also, being infinitely good, presumably is logically 'bound' to do the best thing – which his infinite knowledge enables him to identify without consideration or effort. So why the need for thanks? Praise also (admittedly a 'higher' form of prayer, probably practised little by ordinary people) is similarly hard to understand, given that God can do all things with no effort.

The usual answer to this, by religious believers, would be that I am taking the terms too literally. Of course thanking God is not like human thanks – we use this term because our understanding is limited to human concepts. But really – so the answer might run – our 'thanking' is more like an acknowledgement of the goodness of God and the benefits we receive from him. My reply is simply: 'If you don't mean thanks in its normal sense then don't use the word. Spell out what you really do mean.' But I have no doubt that most people, after receiving (as they suppose) a favourable answer to prayer, do see themselves as thanking God in just the way they would thank a human being – without any sense that this is illogical.

The appropriate responses to prayer can also be puzzling. In the Bible, we have, '*If ye have faith as a grain of mustard seed, ye shall say unto this mountain, Remove hence to yonder place; and it shall remove; and nothing shall be impossible unto you*' (Matthew 17:20). Well, this certainly cannot be taken literally; God can hardly be expected to perform an unlimited number of miracles, breaking the laws of nature, at the behest of any human being with mere 'faith as a grain of mustard seed'. But what does it really mean? Surely at least that faith is highly influential in determining the effects of prayer. But there seems to be a conflict between the thinking here and the idea that when a prayer is not answered (or, at least, we do not get what we asked for), we still thank God because *he in his infinite wisdom knew that what we wanted was not really good for us*! What, then, is the role of faith, if all is to be left to God's judgement? What does 'nothing shall be impossible to you' mean, in that case? Is there not a hint of 'heads I win, tails you lose' here? Whatever happens, it seems that our duty is to thank God. Nothing must ever be allowed to cast doubt on the presumption that God exists and is listening to us.

Another common response to apparently unanswered prayer is, 'God is testing me.' Well, to make a trivially obvious point, why should God need to test me when he knows the entire future, including whether I will react to my disappointment in a way that pleases him? But of course, once again the 'official' response would probably be that we must not take things literally. The 'testing' must not be regarded as testing in the human sense at all. My reaction to that, unsurprisingly, is, as before, to demand that words are used with their normal meaning. In fact, one suspects that ordinary people using this language (as opposed to theologians) *are* using the words with their normal meaning, as in the case of thanking God.

Perhaps a more seriously difficulty concerns the concept we have of God. In theory, he should be virtually beyond human understanding; it should be impossible to 'capture' his nature, so to speak, by human concepts. This is indicated by the use of the word 'infinite', in stating the attributes of God. He is said to have infinite power, knowledge and goodness. (Whether we can really make sense of this is questionable.) Yet at the same time, we human beings are said to be created 'in the image' of God; so presumably we must have something in common with him and there must be something in his nature which we can understand. It seems to me that religious believers oscillate between the two ways of looking at things. When a problem arises, and we need to explain away some apparent 'oddity' about God which casts doubt on the viability of our concept of him, they fall back on the 'God is entirely beyond human understanding' line. At other times he is the kindly 'Father' who cares about us, and, in general, seems to have human emotions about us. For example he is sorry, or even angry, when we sin, and joyful when we repent.

And when we look at the history of the concept of God, it is hard to resist the conviction that, in reality, God is 'made in the image of man' rather than the other way about. In the Old Testament he is distinctly human, and the penalties for displeasing him are very severe, often excessive. He becomes angry very easily, and is prone to order massacres of whole tribes with little regard for the rights of individuals. (Richard Dawkins amusingly describes this God, among many other terms of abuse, as 'a petty, unjust, unforgiving control-freak'!) Now surely this simply reflects the *human* view of that time about appropriate ways to treat enemies. We pictured God as similar to ourselves. As we developed a more 'enlightened' attitude to human behaviour, with a greater appreciation of forgiveness, charity, and so on, our concept of God changed to reflect this. It could (just) be argued that God chose to let us discover these moral truths for ourselves, over an extended period of time; but even so, it is hard to believe that he would willingly allow such a false view of himself to be generally held. What was to be gained by this? The only reply is the usual (and unsatisfactory) repetition of the mantra that 'God's ways are beyond human understanding'.

There are also some well-known pieces of doctrine which seem to reflect human ideas and their development, rather than those of an infallible God. Take, for example, that of 'original sin'. I am not at the moment concerned with the nature of the actual sin, if it occurred at all. What is interesting is the idea that the whole human race – each individual person – is somehow 'tainted' by a sin which they themselves did not commit. This surely reflects an early, primitive conception of justice, now superseded. For how can it be fair for any person to be 'punished', or affected adversely at all, for something done in the distant past and entirely beyond his or her control? The doctrine of Heaven and Hell is similarly unjust from a modern viewpoint. I am not talking now of the extreme, literal view of Hell as eternal, agonising pain – this is probably becoming obsolete, or at least fading. It is the whole idea of a division of all humanity into just two categories which is so unfair and inappropriate, given the actual gradations of moral worth of normal human beings.

These are some of the obvious difficulties with the God theory, briefly stated. But one important thing emerging from the above discussion is that the theory really entails a set of related beliefs and concepts. The concepts and the beliefs interlock, and both throw up problems. Take the apparently simple idea of 'belief in God'. This immediately gives rise to the question, what do we mean by 'God' – what concept can we form of this being? We surely need some clear idea of the nature of God in order to be able to affirm, meaningfully, that we believe in him. So there are actually several problems here. One is the concept; another is how it was formed, and a third is the obvious one of the reasons and/or evidence for believing that the concept is instantiated – that there really is a being corresponding to the idea we have of God.

Then there is the theory of 'life after death' – the view (somewhat implausible, perhaps, at first glance) that despite the 'death' which happens to all human beings, we do, in some way, continue to exist after this seemingly final event. The theory of a life after death virtually always accompanies a belief in God. But again there is a conceptual question as well as the problem of justification. Can we form any idea at all of what this life after death will consist in? Is it possible to have a viable conception of a human being in some quite different state – some altered, presumably 'higher' order of being? Can a human being known only in an 'earthly' state be recognisably *the same* person in this mysterious second life? We must have *some* idea of the nature of a life after death in order to say (meaningfully) that we believe in it. On top of that there is the idea that the life after death serves the requirements of *justice* – which means that a *moral* element enters the discussion. God now is supposed to play a new role – one different from that of creator of the universe. It is supposed that he calls on his qualities of infinite goodness and knowledge to judge us and reward or punish us in exact accordance with our moral merit or demerit. But have we any right to assume that the God we invoke to account for the universe – God the *creator* – also has these moral qualities which are, on the face of it, quite different from those needed by a creator? Some kind of argument is presumably needed to support this.

In the subsequent chapters I shall examine, in turn, some of the main questions and difficulties that have been outlined above. I am particularly interested, firstly, in the features of the God theory which might account for its appeal to such a large number of people. These will *not* involve complex theological arguments which ordinary people are very unlikely to have seen. Then secondly I want to consider the *concepts* which underlie the theory. These must necessarily be based on our experience of this world, so the question arises of whether they are really viable when applied to a different and perhaps 'higher' realm. I think that this question is often ignored, and the problems it throws up are seldom fully appreciated.

We will start by looking at a belief which certainly explains one of the main appeals of the God theory to many people. This is the idea that the wrongs and injustices of this world can be 'righted', so to speak, by reward and punishment in an afterlife. I am going to question whether such a view really stands up to analysis.

CHAPTER TWO

REWARDS AND PUNISHMENT

We said in the first chapter that one of the strongest appeals, for many of us, of the 'God' theory, is the idea of God as a provider of *justice*. We need God, in such a role, because this world is obviously unfair. Good people suffer, bad ones prosper. Some are lucky, have a large share of the world's goods and so on; others are less fortunate. And often this has nothing to do with their *merit*, what they *deserve*. What people deserve and what they get are too frequently quite different.

The belief that all this will be 'put right' in the next world is very appealing. Many people take it for granted that God, who is regarded as all-powerful as well as infinitely good, will see that justice is ultimately done. And since this cannot (or usually cannot) be achieved during our life here on earth, it must occur in a 'life after death'. If there is no God, of course, and no afterlife', the injustice of this world can never be 'put right'.

This kind of theory is very understandable and plausible. Is it really acceptable that, say, Francis of Assisi and Hitler should receive the same treatment at death – as they must do, obviously, if both are simply 'wiped out' when they die and there is no future life? Why do we have such a strong sense that this would be somehow wrong – offensive to our deeply ingrained sense of fairness? Surely our 'feeling for justice' cannot be simply delusory, perhaps a freak effect of evolution? Is it not, rather, some kind of perception of objective truth?

Well, we can hope so. Certainly if it were up to us, we would be inclined to order the universe in the way we instinctly feel would be 'right' – with a life after death in which our desire for fairness is satisfied by an all-knowing, infinitely good God. The trouble is that this theory has many difficulties, not all of which are immediately obvious. One which *is* obvious is the question of whether there is a God at all. And I am now going to look at this question – the main concern of the book, of course – in a somewhat unusual way. I am going to consider whether the introduction of God really does solve our problem regarding the demand for justice. I want in fact to examine the whole idea of reward and punishment. We take these practices for granted, but is this justified? Can we make sense of them – do they stand up to analysis? Are they *rational* practices, when examined in detail? I am not, incidentally, claiming that my approach to these questions is original; but I do believe that the problems inherent in the ideas of reward and punishment are not generally appreciated.

Let us begin by observing that all societies employ reward and punishment. In fact, although religious people always suppose that God behaves in a similar way, the practices clearly have their 'natural home' in human behaviour. A child does something that pleases his mother, and she responds with a 'reward' such as a hug, or a smile, or a present. The child commits an offence, and is 'punished' – probably by the infliction of some physical or mental pain or discomfort, or perhaps simply disapproval. Similarly a criminal may be punished by prison or a fine. If he or she behaves well in prison there will probably be the reward of early release.

These proceedings are all human inventions – necessary, no doubt, for the maintenance of ordered society, given that people in their natural condition are often prone to selfishness, covetousness, cruelty and so on which threaten the smooth, lawful running of our lives. All this is obvious and well-known.

But now comes my first controversial contention. It seems to me that out of these simple procedures, two highly questionable developments have occurred. First, we have erected upon what is essentially a straightforward, pragmatic, necessary human device a complex network of 'higher order' concepts such as 'deserving', 'justice', even 'scales of justice', and so on. We start to feel that when a person has offended, it is necessary, not simply because of the needs of society, but *in order to balance the scales of justice* – that he or she be punished. And the punishment must somehow be 'proportional' to the offence in magnitude, whatever this means. In a further metaphor, we say that, in undergoing punishment, a wrongdoer is 'paying a debt' to society, or perhaps to the injured party. This way of talking is so familiar that it is very difficult to see that there may be anything questionable about it.

The second dubious development applies only to people with religious beliefs. These very same concepts are applied to God and the afterlife; it is assumed that he judges, rewards and punishes us (always with 'perfect' justice, of course) according to the merits or demerits of our lives; and in general behaves in the spiritual realm, which he supposedly inhabits, in just the same way as we do in this world.

But really, do these 'scales of justice' actually exist, in any way that makes sense? Are they not just a human invention? The need to protect society, provide deterrents, and so on, is real enough; but is there anything other than that?

Let us look more closely at what actually happens in a reward/punishment situation. Suppose a burglar breaks into a house and steals various articles, causing damage, loss, distress, fear and so on to the owner. He is caught (hopefully), and put in prison for some period decided by a judge.

Now the key thing to see is that the burglary and the punishment are *quite separate events*, and there is no real, inherent connection between them. This might seem rather an odd assertion. Surely the crime was the cause of the imprisonment. Didn't the burglar 'get what he deserved' when he was put in prison? But what does this mean? In the past he might have been put in the stocks. Did he 'deserve' this? How do we decide what he deserves? Suppose the house-owner captures him and tortures him to death – as many house-owners, in the heat of the moment, would no doubt like to do. Is this deserved? Well, surely not. But why not? How do we decide? A few hundred years ago the thought would probably not have shocked in the way it does now. Our idea of what is an appropriate punishment, and how long and intense this should be varies from person to person and from society to society. There is no such thing as the 'right' punishment, the punishment that perfect justice prescribes, or that which is exactly what the offender 'deserves'. It is simply up to the people concerned to make a decision.

It seems to me, surprising though this may seem, that there is no such thing in nature, in the intrinsic quality of events, as this 'deserving' at all; it is purely an invention of man. There is no link between the two events (offence and punishment) other than what is in the minds of the law enforcers and the original framers of the law. The relationship between the events is quite different from real cause, as we see in, say, physics and chemistry and other natural sciences. True cause occurs when, for example, a scientist combines two substances, and a chemical reaction occurs. Or we press a remote control, and the TV comes on. These events are genuinely linked, by the laws that govern the material world. There is no such connection between a wrong act and a decision to inflict something unpleasant on the doer.

At this point I must stress strongly that I am not questioning the institution of punishment, perhaps saying that it should not be practised at all. Certainly not; of course society needs punishment, and no doubt rewards also. But let us be clear what the true reasoning behind it is. The justification for punishment is a standard, well-discussed philosophical topic, and I would not quarrel with the orthodox views. Perhaps the most obvious reason for punishing is deterrence, normally supposed to operate both on the offender and others who may be tempted to offend. This is perfectly rational. So is the hope of reforming the offender, and bringing home to him the nature and consequences of what he has done. Closely related is the idea that the punishment can be seen as an overt expression of society's disapproval. Finally, a punishment such as imprisonment can prevent, for a time, the criminal from offending again.

In addition to these, however, there is the important concept of *retribution*, and this is trickier. It is probably this idea that leads to the impressive-sounding concepts referred to above. The desire for retribution is natural and understandable; but it does not have the same rational basis as the other justifications of punishment. It is an 'automatic' response, fairly obviously implanted in us by evolution. You have done something unpleasant to me; I immediately feel a strong desire to see you suffer 'in consequence'. We can see why evolution has 'designed' human nature in this way – such a response will certainly tend in general to support the survival of a species. For inflicting damage on a fellow-creature is obviously discouraged if there is a likelihood of its being returned. We rationalise and justify the response by using language like, 'You deserve it; it will 'serve you right'. But, put more crudely, what is desired may be simply a form of revenge.

It is important to see that this desire, though natural and unavoidable, is non-rational. The exaction of retribution cannot be justified by reason in the way that, say, deterrence, can.

To justify this claim we only need to consider the benefits to the avenger of 'getting his own back'. Suppose I have been burgled and I am lucky enough to find out who did it. I then get a few hefty friends to 'beat up' the offender. This is done purely for the satisfaction of getting my own back: I am not talking now about forcing the burglar to return the stolen goods – that is quite different and clearly rationally justifiable. Now of course the beating up may be very enjoyable for me, and it might be claimed that I benefit, in a way, by having this satisfaction. But the satisfaction is certainly non-rational. (It might even be called, unkindly, pandering to one's lower nature!) For, after all, I do not really gain anything by inflicting pain on my burglar. The punishment does not cancel out the offence, or remove the pain and distress that it has caused me; these have happened and cannot be undone. My suffering and his if he is punished are simply two separate events, both probably bad in themselves. For presumably the actual pain (mental or physical) that any person suffers, whether as punishment or for other reasons, is in itself a bad thing, however justifiable it may be for reasons such as deterrence. The normal view, at least if we exclude saints and mystics, would be that pain is intrinsically bad.

Again I must make it clear what I am *not* claiming, for it is easy to misunderstand the argument here. I am *not* now advocating the saintly but in practice unrealistic policy of 'turning the other cheek'. No, on the contrary, I would say that often it is highly desirable that someone should be punished – but for the more valid reasons such as deterrence and so on. My claim is simply that there are no 'scales of justice' that have to be balanced; no 'debt to society' to be paid, impressive and persuasive though this kind of language is.

The claim I am now making seems so paradoxical that I feel it needs a little more justification. Surely what is being denied is the existence of ordinary, common justice. A burglar, say, or a mugger has caused me great pain, thoroughly upset my life; surely it is nothing more than *justice* that he should suffer pain in consequence.

But what pain? That is the problem. When should it occur, and how long and intense should it be? It is the impossibility of answering questions like these that exposes the vacuous nature of impressive-sounding concepts like 'justice'.

Suppose my burglar gets cancer twenty years later. Will this do; will this balance the scales of justice? Well, he might have committed a dozen other burglaries; which of them are being 'balanced', or paid for, or whatever, by the cancer? Will a really painful cancer knock out two or three of his offences? Obviously the whole idea, put this way, is absurd. Also, as asked above, what is it that can link together the two events anyway – the crime or crimes and the later suffering? Clearly nothing at all, other than, possibly, the satisfaction that the victim may get (in practice he probably won't!) from feeling that 'it serves him right'. It is interesting to note, in fact, that a burglary victim who really did get satisfaction from the perpetrator's suffering twenty years later would probably be seen as morally blameworthy!

At this point a word about 'justice' may be appropriate. This concept does of course have a role in human affairs, even though I think it is misapplied in reward/punishment situations. It seems to me that it really belongs in cases where the simpler, more homely idea of *fairness* is often the preferable concept. Young children have a very strong sense of fairness. 'She's had three sweets and I've only had one – that's not fair!' 'John's been playing with the car for an hour – now it's my turn.' These are really instances of *rational* judgements: even small children can usually see (though they wouldn't put it in these terms) that one person's interests should not be preferred to another's without a *relevant difference* between the cases. (Of course, what counts as 'relevant' may be disputed, and can require the arbitration of a wise parent! 'John has just been ill and needs cheering up' – the other child might not *quite* agree that this is an adequate reason!) Now this is ordinary *practical reasoning;* it involves the use of the intellect, and we all engage in it. And it should not be undervalued: animals (as far as we can judge) are quite incapable of it; it is one of the 'higher' activities which are characteristic of *humanity*. The central principle of practical reasoning may in fact be expressed as follows:

> Do not treat cases differently unless they
> themselves are *relevantly* different.

The principle is more powerful than might be supposed; for example, it immediately leads to the condemnation of racial and sexual prejudice. An employer interviewing for a job who takes race or sex into account *when these are not relevant to performance of the job* is blameworthy through his violation of this principle. The child who complains that he has had fewer sweets for no good reason is unknowingly applying the same principle. Questions concerning the distribution of money require a similar approach – what is a 'fair' wage; should men and women receive equal pay for similar work; this kind of question. Or, in marriage, the division of unpleasant tasks like washing up, looking after the children – we all have a strong feeling for what is fair or unfair in these cases. Now we can if we like use the rather grand term 'justice' here, though, as I say, the less pretentious *fairness* seems perfectly adequate and indeed more appropriate. But I don't want to say that the concept of justice is not needed at all – that the word should *never* be used. It is well-established in our language and culture and no doubt will continue to be so. And there are times when a 'big', impressive word is needed. If a man is put in prison for ten years for a crime he did not commit, this is clearly an appalling *injustice*; to say it is merely 'unfair' seems ridiculously inadequate. But still 'unfairness' *could* be used; the two concepts do essentially the same job. The key point, however, is that in all the examples just given, the decision about the right or fair action is based on *reason*. It is clearly *irrational* to treat cases differently for no adequate reason. This applies both to the trivial case of the sweets as well as to the highly important one of racial prejudice. Now this is the true 'home', so to speak, of the concept of justice. The same approach simply cannot be used in the case of reward and punishment. There is no way we can employ this reasoning to decide that a particular punishment (prison, the stocks, a fine) is *the* fair or just one required by an offence such as burglary. The concept is misapplied here. There are *of course* perfectly good reasons for dispensing a punishment; but these involve such considerations as deterrence and reform, as already pointed out. There are no 'scales of justice' to be balanced, and no 'debt to society' to be paid.

I will just make one final point. I said above that I was not advocating the policy of 'turning the other cheek'. And of course it would be quite unrealistic and inappropriate to demand this as the norm. When someone does do this, however – forgives an offence, 'wipes it out', so to speak, without requiring redress – most us find it morally admirable. But why? This is paradoxical if wrongdoing somehow *demands* that the 'scales of justice' be balanced. We certainly would not admire a magistrate or judge who 'forgave' a criminal on behalf of the community: there would be outrage, demands for resignation or sacking, and so on. But this is because punishment really is needed in such a case for the good of the community. In the forgiveness case – which would normally be a personal matter – it is the decision not to demand retribution which is admired. And this makes no sense if there is something in the nature of wrongdoing which *requires* retribution. This point is particularly relevant to the supposed practice of God, as we shall see shortly.

Now what are the consequences of the above reasoning, assuming (a big assumption) that my argument is accepted? Well, in the first place we need to realise that it is virtually impossible to avoid the strong feelings of resentment, and, probably, the desire for revenge, which arise in us when we, or someone we care about, is hurt by a wrongdoer. Long-established properties of human nature cannot be eliminated by so weak a weapon as reason! But what we can do is *recognise* that these feelings are non-rational, and try not to let them influence our actual actions. They are very different from, say, the cool decision of a judge, or parent, or teacher, to impose a punishment for more valid reasons such as deterrence. Remember that the pain of (say) a criminal will not do us, ourselves, any good whatever – any more than shooting a wild animal who has killed a human being will bring that person back. There may be valid reasons, of course, to shoot the animal, and similar justifications exist for punishing the criminal; but these do not include 'retribution' or 'balancing the scales of justice'.

Let us now consider how the reasoning given can be applied to our ideas about God (if we have any). I believe that it exposes some serious problems with the normal religious views about God's treatment of human beings.

A particularly interesting and important question, in any religious discussion, is the extent to which we can apply moral ideas derived from our experience in this world to God and the spiritual domain (assuming that they exist). This is a very common practice, but, I suspect, usually done without much thought about whether it is justified. In a later chapter I shall look at the way we use our experience of this world, probably mistakenly, to form our conception of life after death. But the case of reward and punishment brings makes the same point quite powerfully.

The normal belief of all religions postulating a personal God is that this God will punish our sins or reward our good behaviour in this world by treating us in some supposedly appropriate way in the next life. And these consequences are very extreme. We are all familiar with the notions of Heaven and Hell. We are told that these involve infinite (whatever that means) joy or suffering. And once we find ourselves in one of these 'places' there is no termination, no reprieve. If we are condemned to Hell the suffering will last for ever (assuming that time can exist in the afterlife).

But how can these ideas be justified? Is it possible at all for our practices of reward and punishment, devised in this world to satisfy the needs of human society, to 'transfer' to an afterlife? Well it is quite clear first that all the valid justifications for these (according to our reasoning above) cannot possibly apply in the afterlife. Hell cannot deter the sinner and it cannot reform him; for his life of choice and free action is over. So there remains only God's supposed administration of 'justice'; and this of course is the rationale always deployed. But now the objections given above apply even more strongly. Take the case of the burglar who gets cancer twenty years after his offence. We have seen how absurd it is to suppose that the cancer can somehow 'cancel out' the offence, or 'atone' for it, 'balance the scales of justice', or whatever. For the two events are entirely separate. But this is just what is supposed to happen when we die, and God punishes us (in Hell, or Purgatory) 'for' offences that might have happened many years earlier. Now how can my suffering, either in this world or the next, have any power whatever to 'undo' or 'balance' some totally separate event such as an offence I have committed at an earlier time? The two occurrences are simply unrelated. And consider the idea that punishment should be 'proportional' to the gravity of the offence. We said that the meaning of this turns out to be impossible to define precisely. In any case, how, on any analysis, how can an 'infinite', or at least unlimited punishment be justified, for any human offence? This is what Hell is supposed to entail, on any traditional Christian view.

Of course, any justification for Hell, seen as appalling, unlimited punishment, is impossible, and, probably as a consequence, the whole doctrine is now out of fashion. But this is a fairly recent development. When I was at school the story was that an infinite punishment is deserved because the offence is against an infinite creator! This is a very curious idea indeed, and I doubt if any modern religious apologist would use it. But all such reasoning is apt to appear strained and contorted, surely because the whole foundation, the whole idea of retributive punishment, is unsound. If it cannot be justified in this world, it will not be valid in the next.

A further difficulty arises when we consider the practice of 'turning the other cheek', discussed above. Choosing to forgo retribution is commonly considered to be morally admirable – indeed it was advocated by Jesus himself. But if this is so why cannot God do it? Why is it supposed that our punishment after death is somehow necessary, in order to 'cancel out', or whatever, our sins on earth? Remember that this is the only possible justification for such punishment. Deterrence and reform are impossible, once we are 'in Hell'. As we have seen, the offence cannot be 'nullified', or wiped out, because it has happened. Unless we allow time machines it is impossible to alter the past!

A related problem arises when we look at the

doctrine of the *Redemption*. The theory here is that man at some distant time in the past (in the Garden of Eden, or whatever – the exact details are rather mysterious) committed some serious offence against God, thus setting up this curious 'debt' that has to be paid: some kind of imbalance in nature has been created and has to be put right.

There is moreover a further twist that accentuates the puzzling nature of the *Redemption* doctrine: it seems that *the debt can be paid by the pain of a third party* (Jesus) who is himself entirely innocent! Now how can we make sense of this? We gave the imaginary example above of the burglar who later gets cancer. It is obviously absurd in this case to suppose that the pain of the cancer can somehow be linked to the suffering of the burglary victim – in fact, as already pointed out, if the victim did claim to see a link we would probably regard such a reaction as rather sick. But now let us imagine something along the lines of the Redemption theory. Suppose that some saintly friend of the victim says, 'Look, I don't like the way you're brooding over this burglary, and resenting the fact that the chap seems to have got away scot free; it's not healthy. So I'm going to pay his debt. I'll fast for a couple of days, how about that? Or if that's not enough, what about half an hour of self-flagellation? Would that wipe out the debt? Would that balance the scales of justice?'

Of course the reaction to this would be, 'Don't be ridiculous. I need the *burglar* to suffer, because he did it. Your suffering has absolutely nothing to do with my burglary.' But, strange and incomprehensible though it seems when applied to a familiar situation which we can understand, this is precisely the reasoning used in the Redemption theory. Jesus's suffering is somehow supposed to appease the demands of God the Father!

Can we imagine any answer to these arguments? What would a modern clergyman say? Well, one line that would probably be used is to claim that I am myself doing just what I am objecting to, namely basing my idea of God's practices on what happens here on earth. 'Of course (it might be argued) he does not really punish us, in the crude retributive way that you have represented it: if there is any punishment it is inflicted by ourselves! What happens is that we render ourselves unfit for Heaven, for the blissful company of God, by the actions that we choose to perform on earth. Sinful actions corrupt us, lower us; in this condition we would probably not even be able to enjoy Heaven if it were granted us. We have in effect *chosen* Hell – if we must use that word – which is simply the absence of heavenly bliss; of course it does not involve pain in the crude bodily form that we experience on earth.'

Something of this kind would no doubt be put forward, the exact details probably differing from one apologist to another; there is today no fixed 'official' doctrine on these matters (as far as I can see) even in the Catholic Church.

In reply, I would be willing to accept that this is an 'improved' doctrine, at least regarding the theory of reward and punishment in the afterlife. But it does not appear to answer the points about the Redemption, which is surely central to Christian belief. I cannot see how this can be dispensed with or watered down. And even on the question of reward and punishment there are still difficulties. The main problem is that the 'cruder' version, which I have been criticising and which modern clergymen now want to disavow, has certainly been taught by Christian churches for a considerable time, and it is at least questionable whether this 'trimming', this modification and adjustment of doctrine, to accord with modern taste, is really acceptable. After all, why should God, who is supposed to have infinite knowledge, power and goodness, allow virtually the whole of his adherents to be misled for so long? It is one thing for God to hold back, so to speak, the truth; perhaps gradually reveal it to us as our understanding develops; it is quite another to permit his Church to teach a falsehood. This does not seem compatible with God's perfect nature. What is the point of having a Church, which is supposedly God's representative on earth, if it cannot be trusted?

But in any case, I am very doubtful whether the rather sophisticated 'improved' doctrine that I attributed to an imaginary apologist is really the standard view of Christians, even today. As mentioned at the beginning of the chapter, for many people one of the most powerful arguments for the existence of God is that goodness and evil are frequently not rewarded or punished in this world, thus leaving an unacceptable imbalance in the 'scales of justice'. They want to think of God as 'putting things right' in the next world. It can be a great (if hardly admirable) comfort to think of Hitler and his like suffering the horrors of Hell – that is often an essential element in an ordinary Christian's set of beliefs. It has to be admitted also that most of the famous Christian saints – surely men and women with unusual spiritual insight – seemed to have believed in Hell as a 'place' of suffering. In fact I am not aware that any one of them has denied it. It is surely very doubtful, therefore, whether the apparently crude retribution doctrine, with the 'scales of justice' metaphor, and so on, can really be eliminated from Christian doctrine.

Perhaps it is worth repeating, yet again, my main problem with this doctrine. This is that any pain suffered by Hitler (say), however intense and prolonged it may be, is a totally separate event from the suffering he brought about; and his pain cannot wipe out or reduce in the smallest degree one jot or tittle of that suffering. So is the retribution idea really coherent, in this world or the next? This seems to me to be very doubtful.

Notice also that we have ignored the somewhat different irrationality in the idea that every human being eventually goes either to Heaven or to Hell. For even though fewer people now (probably) believe in Hell as eternal intense suffering, there is certainly (in orthodox Christianity) supposed to be at death a division of humanity into just two categories. Given the actual gradations of moral worth of humanity (we are all mixtures of good and bad, in infinitely varied proportions) that is a very odd doctrine, even on the assumption that reward and punishment are rational practices at all.

What, therefore, should be the conclusion of this chapter? To go back a little, we said that one of the main appeals of the 'God' theory for ordinary believers is that it seems to meet our demand for justice – a justice which is clearly absent, too often, from the happenings of this world. I hope to have shown that this demand is not in fact met by the hypothesis of God. Putting things very briefly, if something is bad it is bad and nothing can change that. The fact that a great many such things happen in this world (suffering, injustice, evil actions by human beings, and so on) actually tells against the God theory in two ways. Firstly, it raises the question (a very old, much discussed question) of why an all-powerful, perfectly good God should create such a universe at all. It might seem, however, that some kind of answer to this problem might be found in the idea that things can be 'put right' in another world – where God will use his infinite knowledge, wisdom and goodness to reward or punish us in a totally fair way. The arguments of the present chapter try to show that this hope – and thus one of the chief appeals of the God theory – is illusory.

CHAPTER THREE
OBSERVATIONAL EVIDENCE

In the last chapter we looked at things from a *moral* standpoint; the theme was justice and the apparent lack of it in this world. God was postulated as a possible provider of such justice. However, although this could be seen as giving some sort of argument for belief in God, there remains the question of what gave rise to the idea of God (or gods) in the first place. It would surely be a mistake to suppose that this idea sprang from the need we feel for justice. When we claim that God will 'put everything right' in the next world, we are already familiar with the idea of God. Putting it simply, people need to believe in God before they can see him as an answer to the justice problem.

So how did this belief come about, and was its introduction justified? For that matter, why should we believe in 'supernatural' beings at all? Is it not surprising that so many people, throughout human history, seem to have believed in beings of this kind? That is, beings which (or who) do not seem to inhabit our material world – entities with no apparent physical properties, who cannot be detected by our senses. Why should we suppose that any such things exist?

Well, presumably it must be thought that these supernatural beings at least have some causal interactions with this world. If they do not, they are not only undetectable but irrelevant to us – they can have no possible effect on our lives. And in fact the supernatural things that have been supposed to exist always are considered to interact with this world. The 'gods' of the Greeks and Romans, for example, were clearly seen as affecting the lives of human beings. They were appealed to for help, and sacrifices were made to them in an effort to obtain their favour. The same can be said of the single God of Christianity and Islam. Believers pray to this God, thank him, praise him, try to do his will, and believe that he can and does have an influence on our lives in this world, quite apart from what we suppose will happen after death.

What actually happens, then, in this material world, which might be said to give evidence of God's existence, and/or that of other supernatural beings?

Well, there are certainly happenings which are *seen* – rightly or wrongly – as actions of God. An example is an apparent 'answer' to prayer. We ask God to make something happen (take away an illness, or help us to pass an exam, or simply give us a fine day for the cricket match), and, to our delight, it really does come about. The natural conclusion of a religious believer will certainly be that God has heard us and given a generous response. So our religious faith is strengthened. There are many kinds of prayer of this kind. Often we need God's assistance in dealing with grief, resisting a temptation, performing a difficult duty or whatever; there is a vast number of possibilities. Any apparent help is likely to be gratefully received, and it is natural for a religious believer to suppose that prayer has been answered in these circumstances.

Another common idea is that 'the hand of God' is detectable in some longer process, such as the conversion of a nation to Christianity, or even the punishment of sin, as is supposed to to have happened in Sodom and Gomorrah. And sometimes it has to be admitted that striking and unexpected things, which might plausibly be attributed to the action of God, do occur. A few missionaries perhaps 'convert' a whole nation. Very impressive also is the rapid spread of Christianity in its early days. Can these events always be explained by 'natural' means, or could we sometimes be justified in seeing a 'supernatural' cause?

All happenings of this kind certainly have a strong *psychological* influence on people who concern themselves with religious questions. The belief, say, that a prayer to God has really 'worked', and produced a result perhaps desperatedly wanted, will obviously confirm a normal person in his or her belief in the existence of God. Even if that person was initially doubtful, and possibly praying only with a feeling that 'I have nothing to lose', he or she is likely to have a stronger faith, at least for a time, if the prayer is apparently successful. Indeed, it would probably seem churlish and ungrateful to continue to doubt that God exists and has intervened in these circumstances.

The important question, however, is whether any happenings of this kind *really* provide evidence for God. That people often think they do is certain. But human beings are easily deceived.

I am going to begin the examination of this question by taking an extreme case. *Miracles*, if they really occur, seem to provide the strongest possible empirical evidence for the existence of God. For a miracle is, by definition, a violation, or at least suspension, of the ordinary laws of nature, and who or what could be supposed to bring about such an occurrence but God? Certainly miracles must be one of the most potent of all the psychological factors influencing people to believe. When we read, say, that Jesus raised Lazarus from the dead, and hear him attribute this power to a 'Father' who seems to reside in 'Heaven' (or at least a realm quite distinct from this material world), we feel that his claim must be justified by the outcome – the fact that Lazarus really did (according to the Bible) rise from the dead.

Of course, there will always be some doubt whether the historical record, from such a long time ago, is accurate; but the interesting question is not whether any one particular occurrence really is a miracle, but whether *any* event of this kind – one which appears to break the normal laws of the material universe – can provide a valid argument in favour of the existence of God. Let us not worry about whether (say) Lazarus really did rise from the dead; it is certainly conceivable that he did, and the important question is whether, given that this could be established as a definite fact, it would give us genuine grounds for believing in God, or believing in God more strongly than we would otherwise do.

The first point I want to make is that what we regard as a miracle reflects our understanding of the laws of nature *as we understand them at that time*. But it must always be possible either that we do not fully understand those laws, or that behind the seeming miracle there are particular circumstances we are unaware of which enable the event to be accommodated, so to speak, within the existing laws. Could it be argued, therefore, that no genuine miracle ever occurs – or at least that no event occurs which compels us to describe it in this way?

We might put the matter as follows. Everything we can observe happens *in this world*. The events we are talking about, surprising and unusual though they may be, are, after all, physical happenings which we can observe with our senses – if they were not we could not be aware of them. And it must surely be preferable and more plausible to seek a 'this world' explanation of such happenings rather then rush to some other world of which we have no direct knowledge or experience.

Moreover, given our present knowledge of this world – its complexity, and the mysteriousness and even impenetrability of some of its laws, (those of quantum mechanics and relativity, for example) – is it so impossible to conceive that explanations might in fact exist for the events commonly regarded as miracles?

Why after all should we assume that our present knowledge of the material world – even that of scientists – is exhaustive? We have only to go back a few hundred years, and electrical phenomena would be entirely unknown. Suppose that a time-traveller appeared in a community of, say, three hundred years ago with a battery and any electrical gadget now very familiar. On the operation of the device he might well have been seen as a miracle-worker! And yet today such things pervade our lives; a power-cut leaves us helpless. We take the laws of electricity, on which these devices depend, for granted: they are a commonplace, part of what we see as the ordinary, non-problematic material world. Well, why should there not be laws of nature – perhaps, say, laws to do with the power of the mind – which are not yet discovered? The benefits of electricity were actually available to mankind for all those centuries before they were used – we simply did not possess the trick for harnessing them.

Another point is this. There is always a limit to the 'wonderfulness', so to speak, of the events which are reported as possible miracles. Take healing miracles, for example. A reasonably common occurrence is for a person diagnosed, say, with terminal cancer to recover. Well, no doubt the people involved with the cure will consider it quite remarkable, and, supposing that they have religious beliefs, the recovery may well be seen as an answer to their prayers; but do we ever hear, say, of a person with no arms who instantly, in a fraction of a second, is supplied with a new pair of these limbs, beautifully designed to be an exact fit for that particular body?

Or take another example, perhaps suggestive of science fiction. How dramatic it would be, would it not, if some large building were simply destroyed, not by suicide bombers or some new, immensely powerful laser beam, but at the instigation of a religious wonder-worker. (The Bible gives accounts of this very sensational kind of happening, which now sound more like magic than credible history.) Let us suppose that, angered at the widespread scepticism regarding the existence of God, our prophet or wonder-worker decides that he will teach non-believers a lesson. He calls on 'God' to perform a very dramatic act, such as destroying a building (it would be emptied first, hopefully!) as a demonstration of his existence. Well, there is no doubt that if such an event did occur, it would have at least considerable persuasive power, for many people, in favour of the existence of God, and it would indeed be difficult to accommodate the occurrence within known or conceivable physical laws. But *such things never do occur* – that is the telling point. We might ask why not.

This non-occurrence is surely significant. The standard explanation from religious circles would probably be that God refuses to *compel* belief in his existence. Well, we might again ask why not, but that is not the main point here. What I want to stress now is that non-occurrence of very 'sensational' events again suggests that we need not abandon the attempt to accommodate unusual happenings in our conception of the ordinary law-governed material world. In the case of the cancer cure – a very typical candidate for a miracle – we could suggest simply that the cancer was wrongly diagnosed. Or perhaps the body has healing powers we are unaware of. There may for example be mental powers that we do not fully understand. Is it so impossible that the concentrated prayers of friends and relatives send out some kind of 'healing waves'? Does this sound absurd? Well it is surely no more so than the powers of radio waves would have seemed to a person of a few hundred years ago. The 'new arms' case, however, is clearly of a different kind altogether. Here 'magic' seems a reasonable word to use – we cannot see any way to fit this kind of happening into a modified view of the natural world. But, to repeat, this kind of 'miracle' does not seem to happen.

It is noteworthy that interpreting an unusual happening, such as a miracle, as the work of 'God' is normally done by people *who are already familiar with the idea of God.* Even if initially sceptical about his existence, they will have heard about this being, and the *concept* of God will be there, waiting and available, so to speak, to be called upon when an explanation is needed. Let us, for the moment, try to put ourselves in the position of a person with no prior concept of God. Suppose that this person encounters some really 'sensational' happening which seems to violate the known laws of science. Would he or she then rush to the conclusion that some 'supernatural' being must be responsible? Would there be a resort to another world at all? This would certainly present some obvious difficulties. For how could we know what kind of entity, in a world of which we have no direct, observational knowledge, might be supposed to have the power and motivation to perform such an action?

This in fact brings us to the really essential point which emerges from the above discussion.

It is an enormous inferential jump to proceed from any happening in this world to a supposed cause existing outside our world.

The key thing to note is that all our definite, unquestioned knowledge – that which is authenticated by actual observation – is limited to our familiar, material world. (I am talking now of *factual* knowledge, not that of mathematics or logic which derives from reason alone.) This applies both to *the kinds of things that exist*, and also to the *causal relations* between these things. And we are attempting, on the basis of this knowledge, to speculate about the occupants of a quite distinct world.

What in practice people do, of course, in order to bridge this unbridgeable gap, is base what happens in the 'other' world (supposing that it exists at all) on what happens here. But that is clearly unjustified and illegitimate.

It is instructive to consider how we establish and operate the causal laws of the material world. In contrast to the case of 'supernatural' entities, there is a multitude of information, openly available via our normal sensory apparatus, which continuously confirms all our assumptions about the behaviour of material things. Take for example a familiar physical law such as that of gravity. We are using this, and in effect confirming its validity, through most of the actions of our lives. We climb up and down stairs, or use lifts, pick things up and drop them, build shelves to hold objects at a convenient distance from the ground, never for a moment doubting that gravity will operate in just the way it has for the entire lifetime of the universe. And always, of course, our confidence is justified – and we are so used to this that we simply cannot conceive the possibility that, say, an object released above the ground will not fall down. Or take electricity and its laws. As already pointed out, we are now dependent on a huge variety of electrical gadgets for the operation of our normal lives. And these gadgets work because the laws of electricity (admittedly discovered fairly recently) can be relied upon to operate just as they have done in the past.

Perhaps even more striking is the fact that our conceptions of the *very nature* of things depend on the laws they obey. Objects are described, for example, as 'heavy', or 'hard', or as 'a good conductor', or an 'insulator'. These descriptions would make no sense if we had no familiarity with the laws of gravity and electricity.

The essential point, however, is that we continually observe *both causes and their effects*. An astronomically high number of instances is available to us as confirmation of the laws of the material world.

Contrast this now with our situation regarding the supposed occupants – if they exist at all – of some supposed 'other world'. How are we to find out anything at all about such a mysterious realm? All our normal means – involving the use of the senses – are inoperative because, by definition, this other world is quite distinct from the material world which we access through our senses. In the case of a 'miracle' our only evidence is one single event in the material world. How can it be possible to jump from this to any happening in a totally different, unperceivable world?

There are really two separate points to notice here. The first is that, in the case of an apparent miracle, we are seeing just *one* happening, as opposed to the multitude of events giving us evidence as to the laws governing this world. The second point is that the miracle is actually just one 'end' of a supposed causal event which must have two essential components: we have access only to the effect. In these circumstances we must necessarily be completely in the dark as to whether there is a cause at all (in this mysterious 'other world') and, if it exists, the nature of this cause. Remember that the nature of a thing is intimately linked to its causal relationships with other things (hardness, weight, conductivity, etc) and we have no knowledge of these.

The truth is that the *psychological* effect of something 'wonderful' – such as an apparent 'answer' to prayer – is deceptive. The psychological effect is strong, but the real argument which follows from the occurrence is weak. To illustrate the former let us return to our earlier example of the seemingly miraculous cure. Suppose one of my friends or relations is diagnosed with terminal cancer and I gather together a group of committed Christians who undertake a sustained prayer session, appealing to God for a cure. We all believe that this 'God' has unlimited power, is perfectly good, and that he cares about our welfare. We have been taught that he values our prayers and regards them as a demonstration of our faith that he exists and has the power to help us. Well, let us suppose that after a few weeks our friend starts to improve. The tumour shrinks and, to the surprise of the doctors, the patient eventually makes a full recovery. Are we not entitled to believe that God has indeed answered our prayers? Would it not be perverse, almost sinful, to be sceptical, as well as ungrateful to a generous God?

The power of this way of looking at things is obvious, and indeed it might be said to be perfectly justified and logical, given one condition. It relies upon *the assumption that God is already known to exist.* And people who pray in the way described obviously will be making this assumption. But in our present discussion we are adopting a different position: we are looking for evidence, or reasons, for a belief that a being such as 'God' exists at all. For this approach we need to suppose that we have no *prior* knowledge of God, or an afterlife, or a 'spiritual' realm distinct from this world. We have to be open-minded, willing to be convinced either way.

For many people this is quite a difficult position to take up. Most of us come to these philosophical investigations with a concept of God 'ready-made', as it were. The reason, of course, is that we have usually had some sort of religious education, involving at least an introduction to the principal religious concepts. And while we may – probably at a later age – develop doubts as to whether God does actually exist, the *concept* of God, the nature he has if he exists, is taken for granted. Now of course an essential part of this concept is his power and willingness, at least sometimes, to take a part in the doings of our world. He can, if he wishes, perform a 'miracle', for this is simply a suspension of the ordinary laws of nature. And these laws are, after all, designed and put into effect by God himself.

It follows that God is the natural 'first port of call' (perhaps the only port of call) when we seek an explanation for an extraordinary event which looks like a miracle. We immediately think of him as a possible cause, and probably can conceive of no other plausible possibility. But, to repeat, in this discussion we are taking a different stance. We are looking for evidence, or reasons, for a belief that *anything*, including God and an afterlife, outside our familiar material universe exists at all. And once we adopt this position things look very different. Is there really any feature of an earthly happening, even a 'miracle', which could lead a person with no prior idea of God to conceive of the being with infinite power, knowledge and goodness that we now understand by the term? Surely not. We could imagine all sorts of causes, not to mention the much more plausible accommodation of the occurrence within the laws of this world. Miracles, and other events of the material world could only – if at all – count as evidence for a 'supernatural' theory already formed. We need *independent* reasons for belief in God before observable happenings in the material world can count in his favour.

A further key point which must be stressed is that in any kind of analysis that we undertake *we can only work with the concepts we have*. Given also that human beings seem to have a 'built-in' need to find explanations for what they observe, we can see why the 'God' kind of explanation is so compelling. That concept is there, formed by tradition and education, waiting to be called upon when various events (miracles, answers to prayer, and so on) seem to demand explanation. We know that more primitive societies, also seeking explanation but lacking scientific training and knowledge, gave very different accounts of what they observed. For example, there was often a belief in 'spirits', often with suspiciously human characteristics. These people could of course work only with the concepts of their own time. People of today, with more 'advanced' concepts, now tend to regard such notions as spirits as absurd superstitions. But we ourselves are just as dependent on the concepts we possess for the explanations we are able to give. That of God – the supremely good and powerful being we are all familiar with – is one of these.

At this point a reader may feel that the ignorance I seem to be postulating about anything other than the material world is unjustified. It may never be *certain* that God is the agent responsible for, say, a cure; but it is surely a possibility, and, in some circumstances, a very plausible hypothesis. It may also be felt that I have given too much weight to what is called the *empirical* approach, and, in particular, the methods of *natural science*. This is the standard (and highly successful) procedure for obtaining knowledge of the *material* things of this world. But is existence limited to the material? God is supposed, is he not, to be a 'spirit'? Might there not be other means of acquiring knowledge of a spiritual world, if it exists? After all, since there can be no material objects in a purely spiritual world, there would have to be, in such a world, some means of communication other than the ones we are accustomed to here. Could God perhaps convey knowledge of his existence directly to our minds? The idea of a 'religious experience' is familiar, and religious believers often speak of 'Faith', a concept which is prominent in the Bible. Could Faith be a legitimate means of obtaining knowledge?

These questions clearly deserve full consideration, and in the next chapter we will continue the discussion with particular reference to the arguments from Faith and religious experience.

CHAPTER FOUR

OTHER ROUTES: FAITH, RELIGIOUS EXPERIENCE

This chapter continues the discussion of the previous one, and will use similar considerations and reasoning. We have now, however, to deal with a rather different kind of argument in favour of the 'God' theory. As said at the end of the last chapter, there seems no obvious reason why God, if he exists, should not convey information directly to our minds, without our taking the more usual route to knowledge which is the observation of material things. This line of thought provides us with a possible definition of 'Faith' – clearly an important religious concept. We might say that Faith is the belief that there are ways of acquiring knowledge, particularly knowledge of religious matters, other than those appropriate to knowledge of the material world.

I should say at once that there does not seem to be any way in which this kind of view could be conclusively refuted. And its psychological power cannot be doubted. The great saints of the past surely did not acquire their beliefs from theological arguments or empirical evidence! They must have had some other source, obviously something along the lines of this 'Faith' we are investigating. But the certainty with which they held their convictions, along with the resulting quality of their lives, is highly impressive and quite capable of inspiring similar beliefs in others. The idea that, say, St Francis of Assisi was simply deluded about his faith, and his ecstatic death was in reality followed by total destruction and no survival of his 'soul', is unbelievable, even abhorrent to many people. There is a strong conviction that things simply cannot be like that. It is felt that the universe just has to be set up in a way which is more accordant with our instinctive convictions and wishes.

We may of course be highly sympathetic to this line of thought, or it might be dismissed as simply irrational wishful thinking. All we can do here is look at the arguments as coolly and objectively as possible, and be aware that there is a strong case on the other side, however objectionable that may be to an orthodox religious believer. And there are unfortunately difficulties with the 'Faith' theory, along with the similar arguments based on 'religious experience', which are not dissimilar to those found in the investigation into miracles.

Firstly, anything happening 'in' (as we say) our minds, though apparently of a different nature from physical occurrences, is still an event *of this world*, and there is a familiar, normal cause for such events, namely physical happenings in the brain. We have ample evidence of this process. When, for example, the brain is damaged, as in Alzheimer's disease, the 'mental' side of a person is radically altered, often distressingly so. And of course perceptual experiences such as those of sight, touch and hearing come to us by a *physical* process via nerves which link the brain to the 'outside' world.

So how are we to know, given *any* mental experience, that it comes from God and not simply from some condition of the brain? The brain, after all, is enormously complex, and we have only a very limited understanding of how it works. It is impossible to say of any mental experience that there is no state of the brain which could conceivably cause it.

Moreover we should not be taken in by a strong subjective sense of conviction, on the part of the 'receiver' of a mental experience, that it comes from God or some 'supernatural' source. This conviction is very common, in religious believers; but strength of belief is never a good guide to truth: unfortunately human beings are very prone to extreme error, often accompanied by a powerful, even fanatical conviction of the truth of the belief in question. We shall look at human error and its causes in another chapter; but, to give just one striking example, it is only necessary to consider suicide bombers to see how a fanatical conviction can accompany a belief which the majority of mankind would regard as profoundly and tragically mistaken.

What could God do, therefore, what kind of mental event could he cause, to produce valid evidence that he exists and the event is caused by him? It is surprisingly hard to think of anything. There is no possible quality of any mental event that can say, 'This must be brought about by a being with infinite power and goodness'. An *impression,* even a *conviction* that 'this is from God' – for a person who already has a concept of such a being, is another matter.

At the risk of repetition, let me stress an important point which arose in the last chapter. Even if – impossible though this now is – we could somehow come to know that a mental event had no physical cause in the brain, it would still be an enormous inferential jump to suppose that it came from God. For, as we saw in the case of miracles, establishment of causal relationships requires access to both cause and effect. In this world we have a vast, unlimited number of examples of ordinary physical laws. We gave the example earlier of the law of gravity. Any object, released from above the ground, falls. This always happens, and we have total confidence that this law will continue to operate throughout the foreseeable future. Less obvious laws, discovered by scientists, are established by carefully designed experiments, and it is essential that these are *repeatable*. No new scientific theory is accepted until it is tested and verified by different groups of scientists, probably in different parts of the world. And it should be noticed that *both cause and effect* must be observable events.

Contrast this now with our situation when we might suppose that an event in this world – even 'in' the mind – gives evidence of some happening in a totally distinct, unobservable world. We have no way of knowing whether causal relations are possible at all between the different worlds. And if they are, what kind of entities can be supposed to exist and be responsible for such interactions. For how can observing only an effect (or supposed effect) tell us anything at all about the nature of the cause; or, for that matter, whether there is a cause at all? Even if we allow the possibility of causal links between the different worlds, why should these be anything like those that operate in this world? And we have experience only of the latter.

It needs to be stressed, at this point, that in the present discussion *we are not assuming that God is already known to exist*. We are looking for possible evidence or reasons for believing in his existence. Again as pointed out in the previous chapter, in adopting this stance we need to suppose that we have no definite knowledge of whether such things as God, an afterlife, a 'spiritual' realm distinct from this world, and so on, exist at all. In the last chapter we looked at *observable* events such as miracles. Now we need to consider whether any *mental* occurrence could give valid evidence of God's existence to a person with no prior conception of supernatural beings. And by a mental occurrence I include both 'religious experiences' – that is, unusual individual events – and long-term convictions such as the 'Faith' to which religious people often refer. St Paul's experience on the Road to Damascus would be a dramatic example of the first kind.

In the last chapter I stressed the importance of *the concepts we already possess.* We are limited to the use of these when seeking explanations. The same point also applies to any mental events which may be thought to have religious significance. We can only describe these using language and concepts already implanted in our minds by education and experience. So when something unusual occurs, it is natural to anyone brought up in a religious tradition to call on their religious concepts when attempting to analyse what has been experienced. Even Francis of Assisi could think in terms of 'Our Lord', the 'Virgin Mary' and so on, only because he had been brought up with those concepts. Had he been born a hundred years before Jesus Christ he would have been incapable of interpreting any religious experience in that way. The Fatima children could only (eventually) interpret the vision they saw as 'Our Lady' (the mother of Jesus Christ) because they had been already introduced to the idea of Our Lady by their parents and teachers.

So is it *justified* to interpret religious experiences by using our familiar religious concepts? Could there be anything in the *intrinsic* nature of a mental event which bespeaks God? One difficulty with this idea is that, to a certain degree, the language we use appears to *determine*, at least in part, the character of a mental event. It is hard to conceive of the event as having some nature of its own which is quite independent of the concepts under we categorise it. If these concepts are not available – if in particular, we do not already possess the concept of God – it is surely inconceivable that any mental event alone, unclassified by language, could indicate a meaning amounting to: 'This must be brought about by a being of infinite power, knowledge and goodness.'

The fact is, surely, that we need the conceptual apparatus, so to speak, of religion, in order to see our experience in a religious light, and describe it using religious concepts and language. But does this matter; does it tell against the idea that God is using this way of communicating with us? After all, why should he not use the means of communication which have grown up among previous believers and been handed down to later generations? For example, when St Paul on the road to Damascus heard the voice saying 'Saul, Saul, why do you persecute me?' in his own language, well, why should those words not come from God? How else could God be expected to communicate with a human being?

It must be admitted, as already said, that this account cannot be rejected as completely impossible. But let us remember also that any mental event, including words 'heard' internally by one person only, could equally be caused by a physical happening in the brain. Important also is the phrase used in the last paragraph, 'grown up among previous believers'. It is certainly true that religious concepts, including that of God, emerged somehow in the thoughts, teaching and writing of the people of the past. But are the concepts therefore valid? Is their construction justified? Many concepts, now regarded as absurd, have been devised by people of the past. Examples, as already mentioned, are witches and evil spirits. We do not, presumably, now believe that these concepts are *instantiated* – that any entities of those kinds actually exist. So are there adequate reasons to suppose that the more familiar and 'respectable' religious concepts are instantiated?

What in fact is the origin of the concept of God? Well, that is of course hard to say. Probably the idea of God, and his nature, evolved slowly over a long period of time. We might also speculate, as in the last chapter, that there is some deep-seated need in mankind to find *explanations;* and certainly one of the principal appeals of the 'God' theory is that he is thought to explain the existence of the universe and possibly the moral law. But let us remember also that a desire for explanation will certainly not always – particularly in the early history of man – be accompanied by an ability to judge a particular explanation's validity. The truth is that when a doctrine becomes established, generally accepted, it can quickly acquire an 'authority' based on little more than the fact that it *is* generally accepted, and has been so for a long time. It is felt that something believed by so many for so long simply must be true. The process by which religious concepts are transmitted will also no doubt involve tradition and education by respected elders and this very process must increase the feeling of 'established truth' which religious beliefs tend to possess.

A particularly important component in the transmission of religious doctrine is that of 'holy books', which are thought to have special authority. And the further back in the past such books were written, the more they acquire a sort of mystic aura, which no writing in the recent past could possibly have. Many people find it quite easy to believe that the writers of the Bible (for example) – unknown, mysterious people from a world of long ago – were inspired by God. It is sometimes even thought that such books could be said to be written 'at the dictation' of God. Certainly huge numbers of believing Christians today – including some highly intelligent scientists – would be happy to call the Bible 'the Word of God'.

To state the obvious, however, in whatever manner the concept of God arose, it was certainly the work of *human beings*, who had no more access to any *evidence* for his existence than we ourselves do. There were no superior means of investigation in the past which are not available to ourselves, the people of today. We should not suppose that, say, Moses and the prophets had any right to teach with some special authority which we now lack. They may have considered themselves 'inspired', guided by God, but it is hard to see how such a claim could be proved. They were, after all, simply human beings performing the physical operations of teaching by means of speech, and writing. The fact that it is in the distant past that 'holy books' were written makes it easy to forget this obvious truth.

How could it possibly be known that a piece of writing is 'inspired by God', or 'dictated by God'? Suppose that a person of today, say a man who is a personal friend and apparently perfectly normal, writes down some thoughts and solemnly informs us that they are 'inspired', that they are not his own thoughts at all but those of God (or some other 'supernatural' being) who is using him as an instrument and dictating them to him. Well, no doubt our first reaction will be to question his mental stability; but if he continues to appear normal, and persists in the claim, what are we to say to him? Obviously, 'How can you possibly know that?' And what could be his response other than to assert his *inner conviction* that God has been communicating with him? And that inner conviction is simply a mental event whose cause cannot be known, but is perfectly adequately explained by some unusual physical event in his brain. The Bible writers could not possibly be in any better a position. I am not suggesting that these people were in any way mentally abnormal, or that the writing does not contain wisdom and insight; but it is necessarily *human* wisdom and insight, and could certainly never be known to originate from God – whatever they themselves might have believed.

It is at least questionable, therefore, whether there is any valid justification for the original introduction (or possibly evolution) of the concept of God. And, to return to the point made a little earlier, it is important to stress that human beings are entirely dependent on *concepts already possessed* – what is sometimes called their *conceptual scheme* – for the explanations they give, including those applying to mental events.

One way to see this more clearly is to try to imagine how we would think about these matters if we had had an entirely different upbringing. Suppose that, like the Romans, we have been brought up to believe, not in one supreme God, but in a number of different 'gods', none of whom is dominant. They all have different powers, responsibilities and areas of influence. Now let us imagine that one of these minor gods is considered to be in charge of health, and has the power of healing. Unfortunately, 'he' (I will suppose this 'god' to be male, for simplicity) is believed, from past experience, to be capricious, unpredictable and hard to please. It is suspected, however, that he is fond of flattery, liking to be praised for his power and generosity; and there is also an idea that he seems to favour the prayers of old people over those of the young.

Well, desperate to help my beloved mother (say) who is terminally ill, I gather a group of my older friends and relatives, and we pray intensively, with large helpings of praise and flattery, to this god. And, lo and behold – after a short time my mother does indeed recover! Can it be doubted that in these circumstances we will attribute the cure to our eccentric god, along with our clever strategy? (We would in fact probably be nervous of questioning his influence, for fear of upsetting him and bringing the illness back!) Now the average reader, particularly if brought up to believe in a single, all-powerful God, will probably think this little story very absurd and just a parody of 'real' prayer for healing addressed to the true God. But is it really? Do we actually have any evidence at all that, in the event of healing, it is caused by our God? Certainly, we prayed to him and the healing happened. But healing also occurred, *ex hypothesi*, in the case of the Roman god. To repeat, it is surely just a matter of the *concepts* we are brought up with. As said above, they are there, waiting, so to speak, to be used when we require an explanation for something that does not appear to fall under normal 'natural' law. And while these imaginary 'human' qualities (capricious, liking to be praised, etc.) do seem very absurd to us now, it is worth noting that the 'orthodox' God, though regarded as greatly superior, is not wholly free from supposed human qualities. When we sin he is said to be displeased, even pained; when we repent (if we do), he is generally imagined to be happy. Also he likes to be thanked for his generosity to us, praised for his goodness, and so on.

Healing 'miracles' do illustrate, in a quite striking way, how remarkably easy it is to be deceived by plausible appearances. A few years ago there was a TV programme in which a person was sent a series of letters instructing her in each case to back a certain horse in a race. The horse she was given won the race an amazing six or seven times in succession and she had no losers. Of course the woman became convinced that the letters were infallible – obviously the people sending them had some source of information that was absolutely reliable. And the viewers of the programme also had the same impression. This very understandable reaction, however, was in fact completely mistaken: it turned out that hundreds of letters had been sent out to different people, covering every possible outcome of every race. Someone was bound to be the one who happened to receive all the winners: we were simply shown this lucky person, witnessing all her amazed reactions when her horses won, and not allowed to see the multitude of disappointed losers. Thus plausible appearances can be radically deceptive.

In fact, though this might seem rather a trivial example, it is in one respect analogous to the more serious healing case, in that for every case in which healing occurs, there must be countless instances where sustained prayer does *not* result in healing. But if we are one of the 'lucky' ones, we will scarcely concern ourselves with the 'losers'. The impulsion to believe that a generous, beneficent God has answered our prayers is very strong. No doubt, also, people who are prepared to undertake serious, sustained prayer are particularly likely to take this point of view. They will naturally welcome any seeming confirmation of their beliefs.

The important thing to see is that there can be no real evidence that an event of this world, however remarkable and difficult to accommodate in our natural laws, is caused by the particular being we call God. And this includes 'mental' events such as a 'conviction', or 'Faith', that God is communicating with us. Even if we think there must be a 'supernatural' explanation of an event, there are innumerable possibilities other than that of the traditional God. We have given one example with our story of the Roman minor god, but it is easy to imagine others. In order for the orthodox 'God' explanation to have plausibility, we need some *independent* evidence, or reasons, to believe that our God exists and that he can reasonably be expected to perform acts such as our supposed miracles. And of course there are a number of traditional arguments which try to demonstrate the existence of such a being. Unfortunately, however, as already pointed out, none of them can be considered conclusive. (If they were, there would presumably be no atheists, or no atheists with the intelligence to follow the arguments.) For the moment let us say merely that neither empirical considerations nor mental occurrences (apparent 'religious' experiences, faith, inner convictions of God's influence, and so on) give adequate justification for belief in God. That must be the conclusion of the last two chapters.

CHAPTER FIVE

Is God a Person?

How do people think of God? I am talking now of ordinary people, and not of theologians or philosophers, And this will include both believers and non-believers, because those who reject the existence of God must certainly have some notion of the being whose existence they deny. After all, I can only assert (meaningfully) that unicorns don't exist if I have some kind of idea of what a unicorn would be like if it did exist! So what characteristics could reasonably be attributed to God?

A reader might be inclined to respond that God is so unimaginably far above anything we human beings can grasp that it is impossible for us to give any description of God. (This is a type of move often made in theological debate.) For we can only use concepts derived from our life in this material world, and God must be vastly 'higher', so to speak, than these. To try to describe him in human terms is to confine him, limit him – attempt, as it were, to capture the infinite by the finite.

Even if we grant this in theory, however, it is obvious that people do continually use human concepts in speaking of God. We say that he 'listens' to our prayers, and 'decides' whether or not to answer them; he is 'pleased' if we obey his laws, and 'sorry', even 'angry' if we sin, and so on. And of course it is completely impossible to have a concept of any being if we do not ascribe *some* qualities to it. Suppose I say that I believe in a 'splunge'. You say, 'What do you mean, what on earth is a splunge?' I then reply, 'Oh, I can't possibly describe him (or it); all his (its) qualities are quite beyond human understanding.' You would of course respond (if you took me seriously, which is unlikely), 'Then the word "splunge" is simply meaningless.' Clearly one cannot genuinely believe in the existence of a being with no meaningful description. And since millions of people certainly do believe in the existence of a being called God, the word cannot be completely meaningless.

God then must have some qualities which we can, to some degree, understand, in order for us to be justified in talking of God at all. What are these? Well, that does not seem so difficult. As already pointed out, one of the main reasons for believing in God is to provide an explanation for the existence of the universe. That leads to the idea of an *omnipotent* being. Similarly there is the problem of morality, the injustice of this world, and so on. Again as mentioned previously, God seems to solve this since he is always seen as a being with *perfect goodness*, who has the ability and power to judge human beings and reward or punish them. So here are two attributes of God.

The trouble is, though, that these traditional qualities of omnipotence and infinite goodness refer only to what God *does*, or is able to do. They do not describe the being which (or who) performs these actions. And we surely must (logically) have some viable concept of God *before* – in some sense – we can talk of this being as doing things.

A simple example should make this clear. You tell me, let us say, that you have just met a person of great moral goodness. Well, that certainly tells me something about the person – I have an idea of how he or she will act in various circumstances. If this person comes across someone who is suffering, or in need, or distress of some kind, I can be pretty sure that he or she will do everything possible to help. But I do not know whether your person is male or female, young or old, tall or short, fair or dark, intelligent, interested in art, music, sport – in fact I can form no clear conception of the person themselves at all. Your description is, so to speak, *external*; it does not capture the *intrinsic* qualities of the person.

So what do we know, or think we know, about God himself? There is in fact one quality of great importance: God is always considered to be a *person*. We speak of him as a 'personal God'. And clearly, if God is to listen to our prayers, perhaps answer them, be pleased when we are good, sorry when we sin, and so on – in other words, feel, think, react in ways with which we ourselves are familiar – then he (or she, or it) must, at least to some degree, share the *personal* nature that we ourselves possess. Another point is that we human beings are always said to be 'made in the image of God'. This again suggests that he (I will now use this pronoun, for simplicity) must be a personal God.

Now whatever else this means, it certainly implies *consciousness*. No inanimate piece of existent 'stuff' – for want of a better word – could make decisions, experience approval, and so on.

But it is here that difficulties arise. We understand what it is to be a conscious person from *our own case and our acquaintance with other human beings*. People like ourselves are the only persons we are acquainted with. (Possibly animals have some personal properties also, but I would suggest that we only credit them with such qualities to the extent that they resemble ourselves. We hardly think of insects as persons.) So we *have* to think of God as possessing identifiably similar personal qualities to our own. Otherwise how are we to conceive of him at all? And now we begin to see that things are not as simple as they might at first appear. Our own personal qualities are intimately linked to *our situation here on earth*, with all its difficulties, problems, limitations and so on which cannot possibly apply to God. There is a clear conflict, therefore, between the belief that God is unimaginably far 'above' human nature and the need to attribute qualities to him which we can understand.

The conflict becomes more evident when we try to think of actual personal qualities which might reasonably be attributed to God. And it must be borne in mind that our understanding of such qualities can only be derived from our own experience. It is in fact immediately clear that most of our own thoughts, feelings, decisions, and so on are to do with what happens to us, and how we respond, in this material world. (Presumably our minds and brains actually evolved to enable us to negotiate this world.) And notice the essential role of the human *body* in this. Our bodies have to be fed, clothed, kept healthy, allowed to sleep, protected from damaging physical contact, and so on. The thoughts we have, and the decisions we make, though themselves *mental* events, are largely concerned with the *physical* measures that have to be taken to achieve these things. Also it is only through our bodies, particularly the nervous system, that we have pleasurable sensations and physical pain. Much of our decision-making involves methods of obtaining the one and avoiding the other.

Now none of this can possibly apply to God, who (on all orthodox views) has no body.

Again, much of our thought results from our *limitations*, our lack of knowledge, particularly of the future. We have to plan things out, weighing different alternatives, making value-judgements on which our choices are based. 'Shall I take this new job? There will be more money, but the children will have to move schools, my wife will have to make new friends.' And so on and so on. These decisions take time, and often need modifying because of our inability to foresee the future. Once more, it is inconceivable that God should have mental processes remotely like this; for he knows everything that actually will happen, as well as what would happen as a consequence of anything that he, or any other personal being, might choose to do. He can have no worries, regrets, hopes, pleasurable anticipation; for these are essentially linked to our human situation with its limitations, ignorance of the future, and so on. God can indeed determine the future himself (assuming that there is time at all in God's world), if he so wishes – though it is hard to see that he has much choice, given that he is perfectly good and presumably must always select the morally best action.

I can imagine now some exasperation on the part of the average reader. Surely these are very trivial objections to the idea of a personal, conscious God. *Of course* he does not have our thoughts, sensations, concerns; he is vastly above all that. But this does not mean that he cannot be a conscious, thinking person; it is just that we are incapable of understanding the kind of thoughts he has. Presumably an animal, even an 'advanced' primate, such as an ape, cannot understand our own human thoughts. Certainly an ape could have no conception of higher mathematics, for example. But we know that such thoughts and concepts exist, and why should not God's thoughts exist in the absence of our understanding of them?

Well, perhaps. This is a superficially plausible line of argument. But I am afraid that it is just the kind of move which is so common, and tempting, whenever a difficulty arises about the nature of God. 'It is all far above our limited human understanding'. And, to repeat, it is essential that we have *some* grasp of the qualities we attribute to God, or what we are saying is simply meaningless. The truth is that we do consider him to be a conscious being, and our understanding of 'conscious' is derived from our acquaintance with our own experience of consciousness. So 'his' consciousness, if it exists, must be in some way recognisably of a similar kind to our own. The problem is that when we examine the thoughts, sensations, judgements and so on that characterise human consciousness, it is hard to find anything at all that sits happily, so to speak, with the usual concept of God. The unlimited nature of his powers, compared with the very limited nature of our own, militates against this.

Let us consider God's relationship to ourselves. However 'high' and incomprehensible God's mental life may be, we always imagine that a part of his consciousness is devoted to us and our behaviour, particularly its moral character. After all, God created us (supposedly) and must be interested in our welfare and moral quality. As already said, we certainly believe him to be pleased when we behave well and sorry when we sin. Also we imagine him 'listening' to our prayers, and 'deciding' how to respond.

But none of this can really be true. Given his omniscience, he must have known from all eternity how we will behave in every situation we experience, and how he will respond. Any 'pleasure' at our good behaviour would surely have happened when he first made the decision to create us; there is no reason why it should occur at the moment when the act is actually committed. In any case it is hard to suppose that a being of the awesome grandeur of God could really feel anything like our pleasure or pain. That would imply the possibility of a condition lacking perfection, a 'vulnerability', as we might put it, to 'outside' events, which sits uneasily with God. And of course he cannot 'decide', at the moment of our prayers, how to respond, weighing up pros and cons, as we should do. All the relevant considerations were known before we were even created, and the decision would be determined then. So, once again, we see that it is hard to find qualities of God's supposed 'stream of consciousness' which are sufficiently like our own to be comprehensible to us.

Another problem is this. God (supposedly) has been in existence for all eternity, and all other existent things were created by him; so God must have existed, or at least have been logically capable of existing, in the absence of all other beings. What determines his 'thoughts', if any, in those circumstances – when he himself is the only existent entity? What could cause one thought to come to him rather than another? We human beings experience a 'stream' of consciousness, a succession of changing thoughts which are largely determined by our situation in the world. Many of these (sensations, perceptions, for example) are not under our own control at all. Does God have a similar form of consciousness? It is hard to imagine this. Remember that any new thought must be brought about by God himself (here there is a big difference between his and our own situation) and also that God is already perfect – there can be nothing 'lacking' in his nature. He surely cannot desire change, for this would imply something not fully satisfactory in the original situation. So what could be a reason for a new thought? And what could be the 'content' of God's thoughts? He is the only entity in existence, so there are no 'outside' happenings to occupy his thoughts. He might, I suppose, consider what *would* happen if he created a universe, or some other entity. But remember that he has infinite knowledge, so there would be no need for reflection – wondering about whether or not the supposed creation would be desirable. He would already know this.

Yet another puzzle is the idea that God is 'good' – a quality always attributed to him. Our understanding of this concept again derives from our situation in the material world, where our actions affect others and have to be chosen with care. Often there is a conflict between our own interests and that of others and we have to choose between the moral and the selfish act. Again, this is a totally different situation to that of God. It is perhaps possible to see God as a person who performs only good actions, but in what does his 'good-ness' consist when he is the only being in existence? That is, 'before' (if we may use a temporal term) he has decided to create a universe, or whatever. Does it make sense to call him 'good' if he merely exists, performing no actions?

Once again we see that to regard God as a personal, conscious being, of a similar nature – at least to some degree – as ourselves, is not as straightforward as we might suppose.

Let us now consider in more detail the *omniscience* of God – his supposed knowledge of everything it is possible to know. On the face of it this presents few problems; there seems no reason why God's knowledge should not be of essentially the same kind as ours; it is simply, one would suppose, more extensive, more complete. However, we should note that, like the previous concepts considered, such as that of a person, and consciousness, the idea of knowledge has grown up from our own life in the material world. It is a *human* concept, and may be found upon examination not to transfer as happily as might be supposed to a being of a radically different kind such as God.

We might observe first that most of our own knowledge is not immediately present to our conscious minds. It is, as we say, stored in our memory, and can be accessed, through some process which is wholly mysterious, by a deliberate mental act which 'calls it up'. (Sometimes, of course, this 'fails' – we search for a word, say, and it refuses to 'come'.) In general we are prepared to speak of knowledge if the item in our memory is actually true and available to us with reasonable ease. (There are exceptional cases, but these are not relevant to the present discussion.) But most of our knowledge is not conscious; we are not aware of it all the time. There is too much of it for this to be possible.

God, on the other hand, must presumably be supposed to be actually aware of all that there is to be known. Any other view would seem to conflict with God's perfection; it would imply a limitation. He surely cannot be dependent on storage systems like RAM and ROM and human memories! And we do not in general find any difficulty with this idea. We assume, for example, when praying, that billions of other human beings may be praying to the same God at the same time. And we believe that God can, without the slightest difficulty, give his attention to each individual person.

When we consider, however, what this 'infinite knowledge' actually amounts to, I think we can justifiably question whether God's supposed knowlege and our own are really describable by the same word.

God presumably can be said to know everything that is true – everything that can be called a 'fact'. The problem is that what counts as a 'fact' is largely a matter of the language used to describe that fact, and the number of facts it is possible to devise by language is literally infinite and extendable without limit.

Take mathematics, for example. There is an infinity of whole numbers (as well as larger infinities such as that of irrational numbers, among others) and an unlimited number of curious (and mainly uninteresting) relationships between them. Here is an example of a totally pointless question which might be asked about a number relationship. Take 15 trillion, raise it to the power of 47 billion and then add, say, 5,263. Now let us ask whether the result is a multiple of 279. (These numbers are chosen at random, of course.) There must be an answer, and presumably God must 'know' it, as well as all the other number relationships, of which there is a literally infinite quantity. For he knows everything, does he not? To increase the oddity, suppose a race of people work entirely in numbers with a base of 17. God must 'know' all the relationships here also. And what about matrix theory and group theory, which are branches of maths invented by human beings? Did God 'know' all the theorems of those systems before they were even invented? What about a mathematical system that is never actually invented at all, but is possible – is logically coherent? Does God 'know' every theorem in that system?

Again, does God know the position, speed and acceleration of, say, one particular atom in the skin of a dinosaur at any one particular moment of time, and those properties of the same atom 5 million years later? Presumably he must. And what about the literally infinite number of universes he might have created but didn't? Does he know all that could conceivably be described about every element of each one of these?

What exactly do we think it means, to say that God 'knows' this unlimited number of facts, some of which have never actually been expressed in language? As already said, it is hard to imagine that he knows them in the way that we have knowledge. Human beings have information in their memories and are able, usually, to call it up when it is needed, using a particular language and concepts invented by mankind. But God presumably has to be actually aware, all the time, of this infinity of information. Can we really believe that this is possible? Well, of course it is easy to say, once again, that God's ways are entirely beyond our understanding. But we do use concepts like awareness and knowledge, derived from our own situation, in describing God; and if these have totally different connotations in his case it might be questioned whether we are entitled to apply them to him.

These are just some of the rather bizarre and perhaps paradoxical consequences of the attempt to apply human concepts to a being of a radically different kind. In this case it seems to be the idea of infinity – arising from the belief that God has infinite knowledge, power and goodness, that is the source of much of the trouble. We have just looked at infinite knowledge; but perhaps it is questionable whether the idea of infinity can be applied at all to an actually existent being. Infinity as a concept resides most happily in the sphere of mathematics; it is here that proper, rigorous analysis has been applied to the notion. But in mathematics the concept is primarily applicable to *numbers*. For example, there is an infinite number of natural numbers (that is, positive whole numbers), as well as prime numbers, odd and even numbers, multiples of 5, and so on. But numbers are not existent things; they are not what philosophers call *substances*. Now of course the knowledge which we ascribe to God is also not a substance; but it must, if infinite, apply to an indefinitely large number of facts concerning substances, such as our example of the position and velocity of a dinosaur's atom. And God's 'awareness', if it occurs, is an actually existent state of affairs. Can we really make sense of this? Can we conceive of an awareness – in the mind of God – which embraces facts which can be multiplied to an indefinitely great extent simply by the use of language? Well, orthodox theists will no doubt say that we can: they have no real choice here, since their religion compels them to stick rigidly to the dogma that God has infinite knowledge. But we can at least admit that the consequences of the supposition are bizarre and unexpected. These consequences must surely cast doubt on the viability of the idea that God is a thinking person of – at least to some extent – the same kind as ourselves.

With regard to the above reflections on 'infinity', it is perhaps worth noting the misleading effects which sometimes result from the *language* we use. We speak confidently of God as an 'infinite' being, and superficially this sounds non-problematic. But it should not be assumed that we can necessarily make sense of a whole sentence, simply because it is grammatically correct and uses words which individually seem familiar and meaningful. Sometimes words are misapplied; the concepts involved do not 'gel'. Suppose someone says to me, 'I have always loved the number seven; it has a delightful salmon pink colour.' Well, I understand all the words, and the sentence is grammatically unimpeachable; but I can surely make little sense of what is being said. I will probably feel (if I am convinced that the speaker is not simply trying to be amusing, or using some bizarre metaphor) that he or she has misunderstood the concepts in some way. Their 'logic', as philosophers say, has not been grasped. Now I suspect that something of the kind may occur when the word 'infinite' is applied to an existent entity. The concept has been properly analysed for the case of numbers and some other mathematical quantities; this is its 'natural home', so to speak. For example, consider the case of prime numbers. To say that there is an infinite number of these could be analysed to mean, 'Given any number, N, however large, there is a prime number greater than N.' We have thus analysed 'infinity' by using concepts of the finite. But numbers are not existent things ('substances'); they are abstractions. An infinite *being* is very different and it must be questionable whether we can have an adequate grasp of such a concept.

To sum up, let us remind ourselves of the essential characteristics of our own mental lives, and consider whether God could share any or all of these. The key point is that our human thoughts, decisions, experiences are intimately, perhaps essentially, linked to the needs of our lives in this material world. Take pleasure as a simple example. We enjoy pleasurable experiences and often go through a process of planning – which is itself a mental activity – to bring these about. Similarly we try to avoid pain. But like all sensations, these are short-lived. Much of our time is spent attending to the long-term needs of our bodies and those of the people close to us. What provokes particular thoughts, and *change* in our mental state generally, is usually some event which occurs, or seems likely to occur, in the body. We need sleep, food, clothes, and so on, and this requires thought, planning, decisions. It is probable, in fact, that the brain and mind have developed their very impressive powers through an evolutionary process whose 'aim' was the welfare of the body. For the body's well-being is of course necessary to the propagation of the species. This does not mean that the welfare of the mind itself is neglected in ordinary human activity. Much time is spent nowadays in study, acquiring knowledge which again helps in the negotiation of our lives in this world.

Now God cannot be reasonably seen as a performer of any of these mental activities. He has no bodily demands and no need to acquire knowledge, since he already has this to an infinite degree. Planning is out of the question as he is continuously cognisant of every detail of the outcome of every possible action. Pleasure and pain, as transient bodily sensations, are equally unimaginable for God. He might be thought to experience something like 'satisfaction' – at the repentance of a sinner, for example – but since he must have known that this would happen from the beginning of time (assuming that time exists, for God), he would have no reason for any new satisfaction at the moment of the occurrence. It is hard to see, in fact, what could provoke any *change* at all in the state of God's mind. A reason for change would surely suggest that something could be improved, that there is some lack or imperfection in the existing state, or at least some reason to prefer a different state; but everything in the nature of God is supposed to be already perfect. The changes in our own mental lives – giving our 'stream of consciousness' – are a consequence of our situation in the material world, with its imperfections and limitations.

So is it justified at all to suppose that there is a personal God who thinks and acts, at least to some extent, rather like ourselves? Does it not begin to appear that God is 'made in the image of man', rather than the other way about? In other words, we construct an idea of God from our knowledge of ourselves. If the above arguments are valid, it would seem that this procedure is fundamentally flawed – too many problems arise when we try to attach human attributes to a being with the infinite qualities God is supposed to possess.

Now how would a religious believer answer our arguments? Well, to repeat, there is always the familiar theist 'defence' that God's doings are vastly above human understanding. Typically a convinced believer will consider it inappropriate – indeed futile and absurdly presumptuous – to think about the processes of God's mind at all. Such a person will be content to have faith and trust that enlightenment regarding things now beyond our comprehension will come after death. And we can always reflect on the lack of understanding of an ape (say) for human concepts and see this as analogous to our own situation vis-à-vis God.

An approach of this kind is perhaps acceptable if one has total confidence, from other considerations, that God actually exists. But if this question is regarded as open, yet to be decided, we have to consider how reasonable it is to believe in such a being, given the characteristics that other believers (of whom there are vast numbers) attribute to him. Now there is no doubt that God is seen by orthodox believers as a *person* who is morally perfect and deeply concerned with our own welfare and moral worth. Also he hears our prayers, considers whether to answer them and is in general good and generous to us. He is believed to merit, indeed require, our gratitude, praise, even perhaps worship. In other words, he is taken to be a being with some very *human* characteristics. I think that the arguments given in this chapter cast serious doubts on the viability of such a view, and thus indirectly tell against the case for the existence of God.

CHAPTER SIX
LIFE AFTER DEATH

In this chapter I want to look at a doctrine that virtually always accompanies a belief in God, and in fact is one of the principal attractions of the God hypothesis. This is the view that human beings, at 'death', do not really cease to exist, but carry on in some new (and probably superior) state. The degree of happiness or pain experienced in this state is usually considered to depend on our behaviour on this earth.

But is there really a life after death? Will we 'go to Heaven' if we are good, or be horribly punished 'in Hell' if we lead evil lives? Or will there be something in between for most of us who are neither very saintly nor very sinful? And what about those who have already died? Are they still 'alive' in some new way after their bodily deaths, looking down on us (metaphorically) from a superior world?

Whatever our personal views, it is quite clear that the issue of 'life after death', with all the related problems it can throw up, is one of the most important that any human being has to face. Our beliefs on these matters can affect our conduct throughout our entire lives. And of course opinions about them differ enormously. Some people – probably brought up in a religious environment – appear to believe with total conviction that this life is merely a preparation for the next – that while this is an imperfect world, with pain, sin, injustice and so on, the next will be quite different. It is confidently supposed that, at least for those who make it to 'Heaven', there will be no suffering or unfulfilled desires – we shall exist for all eternity (assuming we can make sense of this idea) in a perfect world.

Others of course regard this kind of view as absurd. 'I believe that when I die I shall rot, and nothing of my ego will survive', said Bertrand Russell, one of the most famous and eloquent atheists of the twentieth century. And this is not an uncommon view nowadays: it certainly does not shock in the way it did quite a short time ago. But probably most people in the western societies of today could be regarded as agnostic on the question of a future life. They would simply say, if questioned, that it's impossible to tell. We may hope there will be something after death, but we can't possibly know.

Let us not imagine, however, that the question is dead, or unimportant to modern people. It is easy to see why the hope of a life after death is still quite common and continues to be appealing. There is a normal human instinct to cling to life, and we naturally resist the thought that at some future time our lives will simply come to an end. It is difficult to believe, also – indeed it is abhorrent – that this supremely important entity, myself, could be wiped out, totally, for ever, by some trivial physical occurrence such as a heart attack. Surely the real 'me' – which would for many be the mind, or soul – is too grand and important to be dependent, for its very existence, on such minor physical events. And then there are our relationships to other people. It is horrible to think that someone we love – perhaps someone we have known and loved for many years – will be completely and finally lost to us, either through our own death or that of the loved one.

The idea that we shall meet again in an afterlife is very powerful and attractive. (Meeting those who annoy or bore us is perhaps less so – but this possibility tends to be glossed over!) Finally there is our sense of 'justice', which has already been looked at in earlier chapters. This world is surely very unfair. Some of us have unpleasant, painful lives, while others are blessed with health and/or prosperity. Surely this can't be 'right' – this wonderful, structured universe cannot really be set up in such a way – but perhaps everything will be nicely 'balanced' in the next life. Also there are huge moral differences between human beings. As discussed earlier, it is a deeply ingrained feature of human nature to feel that the good should be rewarded and the evil should suffer – be punished for their wrongful deeds, in a future world if not in this. Is it really possible that Francis of Assisi and Hitler can be treated equally at their deaths – as they are, obviously, if both are simply wiped out? This is unthinkable, to many people: the feeling that, somehow, the world simply *must* be so constituted that fairness and justice, ultimately, will prevail, is one of the most powerful of all the considerations that tell in favour of a life after death.

It is obvious, then, that there are many reasons to *wish* that we shall survive death, and at least some kind of case telling in favour of the idea. But can we really make sense of the idea of a 'life after death'? Taken literally and crudely, the phrase is self-contradictory: 'death' *means* the end of life. Well, not quite, perhaps; it means only the end of life *here on earth*. And that surely does not preclude the possibility of a life 'elsewhere' – in a different and possibly higher realm. It is generally supposed, in fact, that the afterlife, if it is a reality, will not be in a physical world at all. The soul is always taken to be a spiritual entity, distinct from the body and able to exist in its own right, separate from the body. So the afterlife will presumably occur in a purely spiritual world, inhabited by our own and other people's souls.

It would therefore appear that any afterlife will at least be very different from life here on earth. And since we, having lived only in the material world, can have had no experience of such a 'higher realm', the question arises of how and to what extent we can make sense of its nature. Of course, one possible line is that we simply should not concern ourselves with this question. My own impression is that this is the attitude of most religious people. They are content to say that the exact nature of a life after death is beyond our knowledge and understanding; but that we can be confident that it will happen, and that, if we behave appropriately in this life, it will be superior – perhaps in ways we cannot now fully understand – to our present life in this imperfect world. The justification for this confidence is likely to be some kind of 'authority', such as the Bible, or Jesus Christ, or the teaching of a Church, which is assumed to be completely trustworthy. We can of course question whether such authorities really are reliable, but this is not my concern at the moment. I want now to consider whether we are justified in such a casual attitude towards the idea itself.

I suspect, in fact, that a little reflection will show that the whole conception of a life after death is difficult and questionable. To imagine that 'I myself', an entity identifiable as the same being as 'myself' at present, will simply carry on living, though in a totally different kind of world, is more problematic than usually supposed. In fact it is doubtful whether we can even make sense of the idea.

What I am going to do is try to show that most (if not all) of the *ordinary conceptions* people form of a life after death are impossible; they don't stand up to analysis. The mistake commonly made, in a nutshell, is to base the next world, assuming that it exists, on this one. That is a very natural thing to do, because this world is the only one we know and the only kind of 'world' we have to go on, so to speak. But I am going to claim that while we cannot say that an afterlife in another world is impossible, such a world must necessarily be beyond our powers of understanding. It cannot be contained, embraced, within any conceptual scheme available to us in our present existence. And if that is so, then the case for the existence of God is indirectly undermined. For it will have been shown that one of the main reasons for believing in him is invalid: he will be seen, as it were, to be unable to perform one of the tasks required of him.

I should perhaps start with an admission and a warning. Some of the things I shall say in this discussion will probably seem childish and silly. I shall be accused of doing what I have just, indirectly, accused religious believers of doing – namely using human concepts, the concepts of this material world, in a context where they cannot possibly apply. It will perhaps seem that I am interpreting words too literally. Well, the answer to that is that the concepts of this world are all we have, and the ordinary, literal sense of a word is the one from which our understanding of the word is derived. It is very common, in religious discussion, to use ordinary words in what is claimed to be an extended, perhaps metaphorical sense. That is dangerous. When the meaning of a word is extended the modified meaning needs to be explained and justified. Often it would be better not to use the word at all, but spell out explicitly the exact meaning intended.

Let us begin by examining some of the ordinary ideas about the afterlife. We might start with the very popular and appealing view that we will 'see' our loved ones again. (People with near-death experiences often report something of this kind.) And now immediately my warning of the last paragraph becomes applicable. This 'seeing' is not to be taken literally, is it? No, of course not – it's a sort of metaphor, surely? Well, that sounds plausible enough, but what exactly is non-literal seeing? We do commonly use 'seeing' as a metaphor for understanding ('Oh, I see what you mean now') but this won't do for the contact we hope for with our loved ones in the afterlife. So how else could we interpret the idea? I am not actually sure that I can form any notion of seeing if this has to be totally different from anything I have learned to call seeing from my experience on this earth. Let us therefore try, at least initially, being naive and simplistic and see what happens if we take the word in its normal sense.

Now seeing at least implies forming a visual image. Normally this image is of course a result of a complex sequence of physical happenings involving light rays, the retina, visual nerves, brain chemistry, etc., etc. And this requires material things, in space, taking a period of time, and the operation of physical laws governing the behaviour of matter. It might be argued that these physical happenings are merely the means by which an image happens to be produced here on earth, but are not essential to the nature of the image itself. But even an image formed in a different way, in a dream, for example, is spatial, and occupies time. Furthermore its character, the description we give of it (a human face, for example) is dependent   on our understanding of real physical objects in the normal material world.

It seems then that any experience identifiable as 'seeing' a person in an afterlife requires space, matter and time. But can these exist in a future life? Well, why not? might be the immediate reaction. I suspect that most people who believe in an afterlife think of it, in so far as they think about the question at all, in this kind of way. So let us consider whether we could still have our organic bodies, and, more generally, whether there could be physical objects, in the next world. This idea can't be just tossed aside as childish and absurd. Both St Paul and St Augustine regarded the 'resurrection of the body' as an essential element in Christian doctrine, and the Catholic Church still appears to accept it as such. (Whether individual Catholics generally know this, and/or agree with it, is another matter.) The idea is that we will, at some point after death, resume, so to speak, our own bodies. These bodies will be identifiably the same bodies as our earthly ones, but 'changed', 'perfected' – if sense can be made of this. According to St Thomas Aquinas (and others), they will, for example, be no longer capable of pain (mental or physical), illness or decay. They will have some kind of spatial position, but will not occupy space to the exclusion of other bodies, or themselves be restrained by other bodies. Movement will be achievable without effort. The description 'a spiritual body' has even been used – though at first sight this seems a contradiction in terms. These ideas are at least partially based on the properties supposedly displayed by Jesus after his resurrection. The apparently curious idea that these 'perfected' bodies are 'the same bodies' as those we have on earth, while displaying such very different properties, is justified by St Paul by analogy with a seed's turning into a tree, or a caterpillar's becoming a butterfly.

I am not sure how a typical reader will react to this kind of theory, but I have to say at once that to me it seems little better than absurd. It is only the fact that very intelligent people have apparently taken it seriously that, for me, justifies its discussion at all. But surely it is obvious that the theory is attempting, and completely failing, to have the best of both worlds (perhaps literally!). It is taking concepts from this earthly, spatial and temporal existence, and transporting them into an alien milieu where they do not belong and cannot survive. Consider this heavenly 'space', for example. Will it be measurable in miles or kilometres? Will it extend indefinitely? Will movement within this space take periods of time, thus allowing measurements like speed, and acceleration? Apparently we will all be able to move at will, with no effort, presumably to any 'place', so it is hard to see how speed could be a viable concept. In any case, what could determine the speeds and accelerations of 'bodies' in this future world? Surely it is not going to be claimed that Newton's laws of motion will still hold. These involve mass, which is usually measured by something like the *difficulty* experienced in causing motion. Surely 'in Heaven' we can't find room for concepts like difficulty and effort.

Again, how will it be decided 'where' each person, with his body, is placed; and will all the billions of persons who have lived and died throughout the history of the world be 'somewhere', in this world, with their perfected bodies, at every moment in time? Henry the Eighth, Julius Caesar, Shakespeare, Mozart . . . will they all be 'there', locatable, identifiable? Will these special people be accessible to all the billions of other inhabitants of this world, or will we only be able to 'see' and communicate with those we choose to relate to, such as our loved ones? What if the ones we want to contact don't want any contact with us? How are these things going to be decided? Will God act as some kind of all-powerful, super-arbitrator? Could 'disappointment' (something close to pain) be allowed to occur in this 'perfect' world? Again, if there is to be communication between its inhabitants, what form will it take? Speaking, perhaps? This will require ears, and aural nerves, and air, and sound waves. Oh, but these won't be necessary, will they, in this superior realm? In that case we are not justified in using the term 'speaking'. This displays the real difficulty with any attempt to describe the afterlife in understandable terms: we have to use concepts from this world – what else is available to us? – and these are simply not viable in the next.

Let us also think a little more about our supposed bodies, and consider how closely they might resemble those of this world. The latter are of course very complex biochemical machines, which grow, and change, and breathe, and have to be fed, and excrete. Will we have to eat and excrete in the next world? Well, eating might be rather pleasant! Excretion, in this supposedly perfect world, is less attractive. And suppose we choose not to eat? Will these new bodies be capable of all the biochemical changes, including growth, ageing and decline which occur on this earth?

Well, no, of course not; they will be 'perfect' bodies, won't they? They will not be dependent on food, and they will be incapable of decline. But in that case what is their physical nature? What would we find if we dissected them, if that were possible, in this after-life? Would these 'perfect' bodies have no biological structure? We are surely not to suppose that all the organs, the lungs, stomach, heart, liver, kidneys and so on would be there, but not operative. But these organs would have no function, apparently, if we had no need to eat or excrete, breathe, and so on. So what would be the point of them, in that case? Making organs which are simply there but don't function hardly gels with the idea of God's perfect creation. Alright, let us say the organs are not there. But surely there must be skin, and external features like eyes and noses. Otherwise what is left of these 'bodies'? In fact, these 'perfect' bodies are beginning to look uncomfortably like those robotic monsters of science fiction, in which the 'face' can be torn off to reveal horrible alien structures underneath! (Except that these heavenly bodies now seem to have nothing at all 'underneath'.) Calling them 'the same' bodies as those we have on earth seems more and more far-fetched, as we analyse the theory in detail. And I have not even mentioned the obvious difficulty regarding persons who die with very flawed earthly bodies. Cripples, small children, those born with Down's Syndrome . . . it is hard to see what is meant by 'their own bodies', when these bodies are supposed to be 'perfect' in the next world.

(I am afraid that many readers will find the last paragraph irritating, naive, simplistic; using the concepts of this world to speculate about the next in an absurd and obviously illegitimate way. In reply I can only repeat my earlier apology and point out that if we do not use the concepts we now have we cannot discuss the question of an afterlife at all. We can merely assert that it will occur and say nothing about its nature. Perhaps this is the only viable, justified position to take up. I suspect, however, that most religious believers do have a much more definite idea of the afterlife, and that 'seeing' loved ones, for example, is an essential part of it.)

To continue, in the light of the above considerations it is in fact quite difficult to see why the postulation of bodies in the afterlife should be thought necessary at all. What function could they have, if the ordinary laws of physics and chemistry no longer apply? The obvious answer is, to allow identification of the various persons, and perhaps facilitate contact with others. But normal contact requires light and sound rays, and thus the operation of the laws of physics!

A problem of a slightly different kind concerns human *actions*. In this world we have some limited control over our own bodies, and all our 'actions', which are observable by others and may affect others, are achieved directly or indirectly by means of the power we have (which is wholly mysterious) to move our own bodies, or parts of them. This is most obviously displayed when we move other physical objects by placing them in contact with our own bodies (probably our hands), and employing muscular power; but more subtle effects – speaking, for example, or smiling, frowning, and so on – require the use of the mouth, eyes, facial muscles, vocal chords, which is also dependent on the control we possess over our own bodies.

Now once again we can consider whether things could possibly be similar in another world. Will we have the same limited power over just our own body? What about moving other things, or persons? (Will there in fact be non-animate 'things' in this world at all?) If we don't have such control, could not this lead to frustration, and thus a diminution of our supposedly complete happiness? The only 'solution' seems to be that we could never desire any change at all, in the afterlife – in which case, what is the point of having a power of movement?

The key thing to see is that all actions in our present, material world involve *choosing* to bring about *change*, and this implies an attempt to improve the status quo – implying some feeling of *dissatisfaction* with the ways things are at present. And how is that possible in an already perfect world? Also a change chosen by one person could surely conflict with the desires of another. Thus what is seen as an improvement by one person will be regarded as a change for the worse by another. In our present life we make *value judgements* which differ from person to person. All this is absolutely integral to our life in this world. Action, effort, work, and the associated moral qualities of duty, conscientiousness and so on are all essential features of our lives here, and *can only exist when all is not already perfect.* But the afterlife – at least if we 'go to Heaven' – is supposed to be already perfect. Effort, change, satisfaction, disappointment, praise, blame, simply don't belong here; the concepts can't get a foothold in this kind of world. If, therefore, there is to be action, and decision-making in the afterlife, on what is this supposed to be based? Why should we feel the need to change things at all? Change requires the *judgement* that things would better in some way if altered. It can be seen once more that the attempt to transport the concepts, values and practices of this world to one which is necessarily of an entirely different kind simply does not work.

Up to now I have been concentrating on very obvious problems concerning matter, bodies, space, movement – and perhaps giving an unnecessarily long discussion of a theory which to many (including myself) is manifestly untenable. Now surely the answer

to the problems raised is not too difficult to find. All we
have to do is dispense with the idea that there are material bodies, and space, and physical laws, in the next
world. Surely the true essence of a person is his or her
mind or *soul*, and such an entity is spiritual, non-physical, is it not? This is not a new, or implausible idea: it
was advanced and defended with great eloquence by
Socrates, over 300 years before Christ, in the famous
dialogue which was supposed to have occurred
just before his death. (This dialogue, the *Phaedo*, was
actually written by Socrates's disciple Plato.) There he
proves, or claims to prove, both the existence of the
soul and its immortality. But it is a perfectly common
and familiar idea that we, the essential 'we', are more
than, something 'higher' than, our material bodies. In
fact we often contrast the material, bodily side of our
nature with the spiritual, and even think of the body as
'at war' with the soul – trying to drag it down to its own,
'lower' condition. Even though orthodox, mainstream
Christianity rejects the view that only the soul survives
death, and the body is in any way evil, the great saints
and mystics have all been conspicuous for distrust of
the body and its demands, often disciplining it ruth-
lessly by, for example, fasting and abstaining from
sensual indulgence.

Let us consider therefore the view (of Socrates, Plato
and others) that the soul is 'released' at death from the
body, to which it has a merely temporary causal link on
earth; and resumes, so to speak, its true nature in a
'higher' form of existence. We can easily combine this
with normal Christian doctrine and talk of the soul's
'going to Heaven' – assuming of course that the earthly
life of the particular person justifies this.

I myself find this kind of view far more plausible than
that of bodily survival. In fact I think it is the only

variety of theory with any realistic hope of success. But does this 'dispensing with the body' really remove all the problems associated with an afterlife? I think it will be evident that this is not so when we move to the next stage in the discussion. The problem of how to conceive of an afterlife unfortunately becomes even deeper and more intractable when we look at the concept of *time*.

Just as in the case of matter and space, there is an 'ordinary', unreflective view of time in the afterlife. And, similarly, this view is superficially plausible but does not (in my opinion) stand up to analysis. This is the idea that, when we die, time, as it were, just carries on for us, at the same 'rate', in our new world, as its rate in this; there is no break in the continuum. One finds this kind of idea quite frequently in literature, notably in Shakespeare (though I wouldn't want, of course, to assume that he personally accepts it). What typically happens in a number of Shakespeare plays – *Henry the Fifth*, for example – is that certain characters who are about to be executed or die in battle talk of their souls shortly 'meeting in heaven'; and the picture conjured up is of these souls leaving the bodies together and floating off in happy companionship to a superior world where time will presumably just carry on indefinitely in just the same way as it does here.

But things can't possibly be like that. The briefest reflection shows that time, and our experience of it in this world, the 'rate' at which it seems to pass, our means of measuring it and so on, is intimately linked to the physical nature of our world. We know from relativity theory that increasing the speed of a body (admittedly to an enormous degree – something comparable with the speed of light to achieve a significant effect) changes the rate at which time passes for that body. But it is obvious anyway that our perception of time must depend on the physical happenings in our brains. What makes a million years seem an unimaginably long time and a millisecond very short? It must be the physical structure of our brains and the molecular processes which occur there. It is surely not impossible to conceive of a brain with a different structure in which a million years seems like a day to us. Again, we perceive the passing of time, and measure 'lengths' of time, by means of physical happenings. Days and years are linked to the movement of the earth, for example. Try to imagine a world with no physical movement whatever, except perhaps for the biochemical processes in our brains which are needed for consciousness. It is hard to suppose that our normal perception and measurement of time could survive.

Well, given this, what could determine the rate of passing of time in a purely spiritual world with no matter? We start to see now the difficulties inherent in a conception of this kind of world. Can there be time at all in our supposed afterlife? Time surely implies change in the things which exist 'in' that time. And everything is supposed to be already perfect, isn't it? So why should there be change? Is the concept of time viable in a perfect world? Remember that without change, it is hard to see how could we be aware of time?

But even if there is some kind of time in the afterlife, it is simply inconceivable that we pass to this new form of life with no break in the time continuum – that time passes, and has been passing 'there' just as it does here. Can we really suppose that, say, Henry the Eighth has been in existence in Heaven (in the unlikely event that he 'made it' to Heaven!) for nearly 500 years? And that those years, that great length of time, have passed for

him just as they would to us. And this has happened
even though he presumably has no physical brain with
biochemical processes. What can he have been 'doing'
for all that time? Well, presumably nothing, because,
as already pointed out, there is no room for action in a
perfect world. He can't have been 'bored', as this is a
species of (mild) suffering; so one can only suppose
that he has been contemplating God, or something of
the kind, in a perpetual state of bliss! As have all the
billions of other human beings, presumably, many of
whom have lived for considerably longer. And this is to
go on and on for all eternity; time will carry on passing,
but never end. The mind reels (well, mine does,
anyway) at the mere contemplation of this conception
of eternity; the idea of time just going on for ever is
positively frightening!

Now surely this reasoning suggests that any existence in another world will necessarily be 'timeless',
non-temporal – there will some kind of existence
without any change, any sense of 'passing', at all. Well,
this may be possible, but it is surely beyond us to form
any conception of an existence of such a nature.
Certainly the idea that we will be re-united with our
loved ones, who will be recognisably the same people
as they were on earth, is looking increasingly far-
fetched. We have now come to the conclusion, after all,
that in the afterlife there is no time, no space and no
bodies. How could we imagine an actual person, whom
we have known only in this world, where the person has
a body which moves in space and passes through time,
in such a radically different state and yet recognisably
the same person?

A further problem arises when we consider the
means of communication we are to have with other
persons, or souls, in the afterlife. This obviously can't

be achieved by speaking, looking, hearing, touching, if we accept the impossibility of physical bodies – so what are we left with? Thought transmission? But even thoughts, as we are acquainted with them here on earth, take place within time. Can we conceive of time-less, non-temporal thoughts? In any case, thought transmission implies choice and action. We have to choose which thought to transmit, make a decision to transmit it, and actually do the transmitting. And even if the concept of an action is viable in a spaceless and timeless world, we have already seen that there are difficulties regarding the motivation there could be to make changes, in a perfect world. Choice to commit an action, after all, implies a belief that things will be *better*, preferable, in some way, if the action is performed. But how can perfection be bettered?

Is it possible at all to form viable conceptions of other people and suppose that we will be able to relate to them, in a future life? (Remember that one of the main attractions of the theory of an afterlife is the thought that we will be re-united with our loved ones.) What recognisable qualities will they have, bearing in mind that they must be non-physical? Well, perhaps it is unfair to expect a full answer to this question – our understanding of the afterlife is necessarily limited. But I do think we can see the near-impossibility of supposing that we will have relationships with persons, or souls, who are *recognisably the same persons* as any that we have known on earth. This emerges when we actually think about the qualities of real people who are familiar to us now, in this material world. The problem is in fact the same as that outlined above regarding the attempt to transport the concepts of this world to an afterlife. It seems that every one of the qualities of any person we can describe is necessarily, indissolubly linked to this world and the spatial and temporal laws which govern it.

Let us just try to form a picture of any person we know well, and consider the important qualities of that person. Obviously there are physical features, which in this context are the least interesting because they are so transitory – many of them change radically even throughout this life. But what about character, moral qualities and so on? These seem much better candidates for properties of the 'real' person, if there is such a thing. If we believe that the mind or soul constitutes the real essence of a human being, and might possibly survive death, then surely these properties of character will stay with the person in his or her afterlife. But what sort of properties are we talking about? Well, let us suppose that our person is usually described as *generous*, *caring* and *compassionate*. What does this actually mean? Surely that he or she is willing to take the appropriate *actions* to help other people who have *problems*, *needs*. But these needs will not exist in a perfect, heavenly world, and we have seen that actions involve choice and decision to change things, which can surely only happen if some preference for a different state of affairs is present. The same reasoning is easily seen to apply to any qualities of this kind that we find in people. *Selfishness* – a tendency to prefer *actions* favouring oneself rather than ones helping others. *Avarice* – a desire for worldly possessions. *Laziness* – a reluctance to *act* when action is needed. *Sympathy and empathy* with others – these might not involve action so directly, but they imply a recognition of the suffering, or problems, of others, which again could hardly exist in a perfect world. Or take the tastes and preferences of a person. He or she loves music, or cricket. Music involves physical vibrations, ears, auditory nerves, and takes place in time – as does cricket. One cannot imagine timeless and spaceless music or cricket. Furthermore cricket is a *competitive* game; and competition, trying to do better than others, surely could not occur in a perfect world. I am sadly afraid that the vision of Heaven formed (no doubt jokingly) by Neville Cardus – watching cricket at Lords on a sunny afternoon with Mozart playing in the background – is conceptually impossible, unfortunate though that is.

It might be argued that all the qualities of a person that I have described are inessential to the true nature of the person. There is some kind of personal 'substance' – the soul, perhaps, which endures through all possible changes in external qualities and behaviour, and this is the real person. And, after all, a person at ten years old is very different indeed – in appearance, tastes, behaviour, even moral qualities – from that individual at fifty. But he or she is certainly the same human being – there is something which endures through all the changes. So why should not a person be very different in behaviour, taste and so on in heaven, and yet be recognisably the same person?

Well, perhaps. So the man who loves football, and his pint of beer, and a good meal, and his wife and children and a lazy lie-in on Sundays will discover in heaven that his true happiness lies in . . . well, what? Eternal contemplation of the goodness of God? I find that I struggle with this idea. In any case the man *as I know him on earth* – if he is one of my friends – is characterised by all those 'external' properties which manifest themselves to me. Including moral qualities, of course. They are what that person is, to me. That is how I identify him and think of him. The supposed internal 'core' person, the soul which is the 'real' him, is not apparent, other than as it is manifested in his external qualities. And that is so for all my friends, loved ones and acquaintances, however well I know them.

For myself, I find that when I consider any person whatever, however fine and admirable – even 'other-worldly' – their character may be, I simply cannot conceive how that person, *recognisably the same individual,* could possibly exist in any kind of afterlife that I find believable. I can see these people in *another world like this one,* and this is the usual way an afterlife is conceived, no doubt because, as we have seen, it is only in a world like this that a person's qualities make sense – are conceptually possible. This kind of world is the natural home of human qualities as we know them, and we can't just casually move them across to a totally different kind of world – at any rate without incurring apparently intractable logical and conceptual difficulties. So if there could be an afterlife in a world of the same kind as this, all might be comparatively well. The trouble is that another world like this is incompatible with all the usual doctrines regarding afterlives. The postulation of 'Heaven', with its absence of imperfections, unfulfilled desires, pain, and so on; the concept of 'eternity'; the survival of the soul without the body, in fact all the usual views that commonly attend theories about lives after death, inevitably lead, as we have seen, to the problems and difficulties outlined above.

We can of course dismiss all our problems with the blanket panacea 'solution' that the whole thing is beyond our understanding – we must just wait and see what the afterlife will be like. We can't grasp its exact nature, but animals and small children can't understand algebra, and a person blind from birth can't know what colours are like; but that doesn't justify them in rejecting these notions as impossible. Let us just trust the word of God, as we find it, say, in the Bible, and perhaps the dogmas of the Church which Jesus Christ may be supposed to have founded.

Of course, an obvious problem with this is that there is no way to know that any book written by human beings, such as the Bible, really is 'the word of God'. And 'the dogmas of the Church', along with similar claims to special knowledge, are in reality of course simply the works of men. We have made the same point about supposed 'authorities' earlier in the book. Still, I do not want to say that this way of looking at things can be dismissed out of hand; there are no doubt many matters which are beyond human understanding. Nor do I claim that life after death should be rejected as completely impossible; that would be absurdly arrogant. What I object to is the tendency to form notions of this future life which really do seem to be impossible – based as they are on an illegitimate 'transfer' of concepts from this world to an entirely different form of existence. I believe that the ordinary, unreflective view of the character of 'life after death' does not stand up to analysis. And, in particular, the hopes which religious people have of this supposed life, which give the 'God' theory much of its appeal, cannot be met. If the arguments I have given are accepted, then the conclusion once more must be that the case for the existence of God is indirectly undermined.

CHAPTER SEVEN
GOD THE CREATOR

I should perhaps warn the reader that this chapter (the shortest in the book) is probably the most demanding and philosophically taxing. The central argument of the chapter, however, is of key importance to the question of God's existence. The reasoning given might at first strike the reader as bizarre and perhaps implausible; even so, I would ask for it to be considered carefully and with an open mind.

We said in the first chapter that one of the main reasons why people believe in God is that they feel a need for an explanation of the existence of the universe. And it is generally supposed that God supplies this explanation because one of his attributes, or qualities, is that of *infinite power*. We thus have a simple, or apparently simple, solution which seems to solve the problem at a stroke. But does the solution really 'work' when examined closely? In the present chapter I want to show that this is at least very doubtful.

If we reject the 'God' theory, it seems that we must accept the universe itself (or the multiverse, or whatever) as a 'brute fact'. Bertrand Russell, among others, took this view. And it seems that, whatever theory we adopt, we cannot avoid *some* facts of this 'brute' kind, that is ones which are basic and incapable of explanation. For (to repeat what was said in Chapter 1), suppose that fact A is explained by fact B, and B by C, and so on. There must surely be an end to this sequence, and that would seem to require some facts which must simply be accepted as true and that is all. If further explanation were possible there would be other candidates for 'brute' status further down the line, so to speak. But there surely cannot be an infinity of existent states of affairs each serving as an explanation of other happenings.

Now is the 'God' hypothesis a preferable theory to the 'universe as brute fact' view? It certainly seems to be simple and elegant: we have just one supreme being instead of the enormously complicated multiplicity of objects and happenings which constitute the universe. But does a God conceived in this way really stand up to analysis?

The whole idea of 'infinite power' is in fact rather curious and difficult to define precisely. Does it mean simply that whatever God wills comes about? Well, clearly he cannot do what is *logically impossible* – such as making a square circle or turning 12 into a prime number. And people have invented (sometimes rather silly) demands of God such as making a stone which is too heavy for God himself to lift. In this kind of case there is built into the demand something that makes it inherently impossible, and even God cannot be expected to do the impossible. But let us not get embroiled in this kind of philosophers' debate: for our purposes it is sufficient that God should have *the power to create universes*. This is a large enough claim. Before considering it, however, I want to look at the idea of power itself. Perhaps surprisingly, this concept, like that of infinite power, is not as simple as it might at first seem.

We talk of 'power' as an attribute of God as if it were something clearly understandable and recognisable. It

is of course always treated as an essential but unproblematic part of our concept of God. But in actual fact
we do not observe power itself at all. We see only its
supposed effects. Power might even be said to be
something superimposed on a situation by human
beings. To illustrate this, let us look at a simple
example.

A magnet's 'power to attract' means that when a
piece of metal is placed near the magnet the metal
moves towards it, or at least experiences a pull
towards it. That is all that actually happens. If there is
some 'power' behind the scenes, so to speak, it is not
observable. And where does this supposed 'power'
actually reside? Well, in the magnet, presumably. But
why should we not say that it is located in the piece of
metal? This could be said to have the power to move
towards the magnet when placed near it, or to
make the magnet move if it itself is kept stationary. Or
perhaps we could say that the power is in the pair of
objects – they share the power, as it were. Perhaps this
is the most natural description, if we insist on talking
of power at all. But in any case the concept of power
is clearly elusive. I want to suggest that in reality it is
not a necessary concept at all. The situation is quite
adequately described by saying that when a magnet
and a piece of metal are close to each other they move
towards each other. (Or, if restrained, each is sub-
jected to a force towards the other.) That is what we
observe. The physical law, in essence, has the form,
'Event A is followed by event B', and each of these
events is observable, either by our senses or by those
senses assisted by scientific apparatus. The concept of
'power' is thus redundant, and justified only as a
short-cut – a way of simplifying our description of
what occurs.

I should perhaps say that this account would be described by some philosophers as 'positivistic', that is placing too much emphasis on what can be *observed* by human beings. It might be conjectured that there is something 'behind' what we can actually observe which explains things more adequately. What we call 'power' may be of this kind. It might be for example an unobservable property of a magnet which brings about the attraction we observe. Well, it may be granted that this idea is difficult to refute. But we can at least agree that this 'something' is mysterious, elusive, difficult to describe, while what we observe is definite. Certainly we would only ascribe power to the magnet (or the object) if the observable event occurred; that is essential. The presence of something unobservable can only be speculative.

Let us now consider the case of God. To solve our problem of the existence of the universe we need an account something like this. God decides to create a universe (or anything else that is not inherently impossible) and performs, let us say, an *act of will*. (We need not worry too much about the adequacy of this description: he certainly must take some kind of step which he would not take if he had decided otherwise.) The universe then springs into being, out of nothing. That is what 'God's power' really amounts to. Put like that the theory sounds bizarre, if not incredible; but this is essentially the theist position. And we should not of course dismiss it simply because it seems at first sight to be implausible. After all, God's attributes and abilities are supposed to be unimaginably greater than anything our limited minds can compass.

But once we stop describing what happens in terms of God's 'power', I think the account does present insuperable difficulties. The key point is this. *The fact that a certain state of God is followed by a happening 'outside' God has to be a brute fact about reality which cannot be explained by God's own nature.* Oddly enough, God himself cannot be responsible for the happening, in any normal sense, at all. He can only be, in essence, an observer of something that must be beyond his control. He is in the same position as any other observer of an apparently linked sequence of events.

This will seem, at first, an incredible claim. Of course God *must* be responsible for everything that happens – that is an essential part of our conception of God. He has the ability to bring about anything he chooses, including the existence of universes. That is all that needs to be said.

This sounds simple enough, but in fact is not. Just *how* is it supposed that God creates a universe? We said above that he performs an 'act of will', and some readers may object to this, regarding it as too closely based on human behaviour. But the exact nature of God's 'action' does not really matter – the key point is that there must be *some* difference between a state of God which is followed by the springing into being of a universe, and a state which is not so followed. And the change is *in God*! It is he who makes the decision or fails to make the decision; that is where the key difference lies – the difference between creating and not creating a universe. Otherwise what does it mean to say that it is God who is the creator? If something then happens which is 'outside' God – not describable purely by reference to him – then the fact that this happens has to be a property of reality generally; it cannot be 'built in', as it were, to the concept of God himself.

Perhaps the following argument will make this clearer. Whatever state God puts himself into, when he decides to create a universe – even if this simply amounts to his taking the decision that the universe is to come about – it must be *logically* possible that the planned universe does not, in fact, spring into being. Any impossibility that could be assigned here cannot be logical. For there is no difficulty whatever in *conceiving* – imagining, if that term makes things clearer – that the creation does not occur. Thus our *conception* of God cannot include the springing into being of universes.

This point is particularly important and will probably provoke strenuous opposition. Surely our conception of God does include the requirement that if he decides to create a universe, that universe *must* spring into being. That is what it means to say that God has infinite power.

To answer this objection, we might look at the matter as follows. Unless we take a 'pantheist' position, in which God and the universe are seen, in some mysterious way, as a single entity, God must be a being which is distinct from the universe. If he were not he could not be said to create the universe. For he must have existed before (in some sense) the universe came into being in order to create it, and it must therefore always be conceivable, imaginable, for him to exist in the absence of the universe. Now if that is so, it must clearly be *conceivable*, or *logically* possible, for a universe to fail to exist, or fail to come into existence, when God performs the act of will (or whatever) in which creation consists.

This does not mean that there cannot be a being appropriately described as 'God' who can create universes. It can still be claimed that it is *factually* impossible for God to perform his 'act of will' and for a universe to fail to come about. What is meant by this 'factual impossibility'? To make it clearer let us take the example of gravity once more. It is factually impossible, given the nature of our universe, that objects close to the earth will fail to fall when released. But this is not logical impossibility – the kind of very strong impossibility which prevents a brother or father from being female, or 100 from being a prime number. It is very easy to *imagine* a body failing to fall, or even the law of gravity itself ceasing to operate throughout the universe.

Now if this is so then the springing into being of universes cannot be an essential component of the internal, or intrinsic nature of God. If it were it would be impossible even to conceive that God could will a universe without its coming into existence. And, given this, the creative power of God, if it exists, can only be a brute fact about reality itself. It must be a fact *about* God, 'external', so to speak, to his intrinsic nature. And he himself can therefore only observe this property of reality as any other conscious being might observe it.

Again this will no doubt seem highly paradoxical, and indeed demeaning to God as normally conceived. For God is surely responsible for all that happens, is he not? So why cannot we say that he himself is the source of this ability to produce universes?

The problem here is that if God himself brings about his own power, it must be possible to conceive of a God who does not possess the power. He can hardly bring the power about if he himself cannot be conceived to lack it. In other words there would have to be a kind of 'prior' God to the all-powerful one we are familiar with. And this is very odd since it is surely an essential component of our conception of God that he is all-powerful. But even if we ignore that problem, or paradox, how do we explain this new 'power to produce power'? The difficulty outlined above is still there, just pushed back a stage. For now it has to be a brute fact about reality that when a God lacking total power decides to confer that power on himself, it comes about.

A slightly different way of presenting the argument is to note that even God cannot be responsible for his own nature. That he should be so responsible is surely an incoherent notion, for again it would require a 'prior' God lacking that nature.

It is in fact the language normally used – particularly that involving the concept of 'power' – which masks the difficulty inherent in our normal conception of God. God is said to have 'infinite power', that is all. And this sounds, superficially, quite straightforward and unproblematic. We push everything into the internal, intrinsic nature of God – power is just an attribute of his, as being 'square', or 'two feet long' might be attributes of a physical object. But, as we have just seen, this cannot be so, for if it were it would be impossible even to *conceive* that a universe should fail to materialise when God wills it. And this clearly is conceivable.

I can imagine that many readers will still find this analysis unacceptable. A typical reaction might be: 'Can't you understand that *everything* derives from God? You talk of brute facts about reality. But if reality is like that then it is *God* who makes it that way!'

The trouble with this is that this supposed 'making' is just a re-statement of the 'power' fallacy. We see God as able to apply some mysterious 'force' that 'compels' things to happen when he wills them. We imagine an identifiable 'something' in his intrinsic nature which makes things happen. Thus even the ability to make universes is taken to be somehow a part of God's intrinsic nature.

But what is the nature of the 'compulsion' that is supposed to occur when God decrees that something shall come into existence? What kind of 'necessity' is involved. The strongest form of necessity is what we referred to above – which is called *logical*. That is, to use the same example, the kind of necessity that compels a brother or father to be male. In this case the 'compulsion' is a simple consequence of the meanings of the words. But, to repeat what has already been said – and the point is so important that I think the repetition is excusable – that cannot be the case here. We can't explain God's power by the meanings of words, defining it into existence, so to speak. Any 'necessity' in the creative process can only be factual – of the same kind as is possessed by physical laws such as that of gravity.

Let us try a simple thought experiment. A man discovers that he seems to possess some curious and highly unusual power, such as, say bending spoons and other small metal objects. He finds that if he concentrates hard on a particular spoon (say), visualises it bending, 'wills' it to bend, and so on, it does indeed seem slightly to bend. By trial and error he refines his methods, and becomes more 'skilled', more 'expert', in the art of bending spoons. He gets them to bend further, and more rapidly. Eventually he is sufficiently confident in the reliability of his procedure to display the strange ability to friends, or even to give public performances.

Now in these circumstances it would be natural to say, would it not, that this man has 'the power to bend spoons'? That is the way the world generally would see the matter.

But is this really accurate? I would suggest that a more appropriate account would be to say that this man has discovered something in nature, some property of the material world, which was hitherto unknown. A certain mental event seems to have some kind of causal link to some nearby physical objects. Critically, he himself has no more control over this than anyone else; he has learned to produce the appropriate mental event, that is all. How this results in the spoon-bending is as mysterious to him as to others: he is an observer of something 'external' to himself and independent of him. He has learned the trick of harnessing a natural property, just as the early researchers into electricity gradually learned how to harness the properties which are now so familiar, and had always existed, but were unavailable to us owing to our ignorance.

After all, it is inconceivable that this 'power', if we choose to use that term, should be limited to a single person. It must be the case that if other people, or at least some other people – those with a similar genetic make-up, perhaps – should succeed in reproducing the same or a sufficiently close mental state, a similar result should follow. The law would be some kind of general relationship between the mental and the physical, not yet fully understood – rather as electrical laws were not understood a fairly short time ago.

And of course the man himself, who happened to discover this law, need not be exceptional in any way – in fact he would only possess a 'power' which is accessible to anyone else, or anyone capable of producing a similar mental state. He would have no control over this 'power' – if it disappeared he would have no understanding of what had happened and no ability to bring it back. That is why speaking of his 'power' is misleading: in reality he has merely learned to 'tap into' a property of nature which exists in its own right.

The conclusion must be that if universes really do spring into being at the behest of God, then that is a brute fact about reality which has to be simply accepted without further explanation – it is just 'the way things are'. It is difficult to see, therefore, why the God hypothesis should be considered to be preferable to the view that the universe itself is just a brute fact. The God theory has no more explanatory ability. This is because, as we have seen, the power of God, if it exists, cannot be explained by the intrinsic nature of God.

There is just one final point. It is sometimes claimed that God, unlike the ordinary material things we are familiar with, has *necessary* existence. That is, it is impossible that God should fail to exist. (Ordinary objects, which merely *happen* to exist, and could fail to do so without contradiction, are said to be *contingent*.) I do not think that this idea has any real validity; indeed I doubt if we can even make sense of the supposed 'necessary' existence; but it is worth noting that the above arguments are not affected by the supposition. Even if God's existence can be said, in some sense, to be necessary, it still has to be an independent brute fact that what he wills comes about – if this is actually the case. Again, therefore, we see that the 'God' theory has no more explanatory power than the 'universe as brute fact' view.

CHAPTER EIGHT

THE POWER OF BELIEF

I want now to approach the God theory from a somewhat different angle, and try to see why, despite so many objections to it, the theory has such a strong and persistent hold over a large section of humanity. I think that to understand this we need to look at the phenomenon of *belief* itself, in a general way.

There are two aspects to such an enquiry. First, we need to consider the power – a very considerable power – which belief has in governing human behaviour. I do not think it is often realised how strongly our beliefs – at least the important, fundamental ones – affect our thoughts and actions. Secondly we need to look at the ways in which these beliefs are established, and try to see why they can sometimes be almost impossible to overthrow. It is here that we might find the key to the power of religion and its enormous influence on the values and actions of human beings throughout history.

Looking at the matter in a cool, impartial way – as far as that is possible – it must surely be admitted that belief in God is a very odd phenomenon. The oddity is masked by the prevalence, the normality, of religious belief. Whether or not we ourselves are believers, we cannot escape the manifestations, the 'trappings', of religion – these are present throughout our lives. There are still a great many church buildings, religious ministers, regular worshippers; together with ceremonies such as christenings, marriages, funerals, all of which usually take place in churches. Then there are the huge institutions such as the Catholic Church, Islam and so on, with their world-wide power and influence. It is also worth pointing out, obvious though this no doubt is, that there is nothing 'cranky', or fanatical, about most believers; the members of the various Churches do not hold views now seen as absurd, such as alchemy, or belief in wicked spirits – typically these people are perfectly normal and sane, often quite admirable in character. All this subtly influences our attitude to religion; we see doctrines such as Christianity as standard, unremarkable, which, whether true or not, must surely be supported by plausible arguments.

But suppose that religious belief were not so common. Would its ideas and doctrines then seem plausible – in their own right, so to speak? Let us try another simple thought experiment and suppose that we live in a world where there are no churches and ministers and our parents have brought us up simply to deal with the needs and problems of this world, with no mention of God or a life after death. Then after living in this way for some years we hear, perhaps as young adults, that there are people who hold beliefs about a being called 'God' who inhabits a 'spiritual' realm quite distinct from this material world, and who created our universe. We are also told that the 'death' which we have observed to overtake all living things, and has always seemed so final, is not in fact the end of life for human beings. After our apparent deaths we also will pass to a 'spiritual' state. This will (necessarily) be very different from our 'material' condition in this world, but – puzzling though this seems – we will still be recognisably the same people as we are now. Furthermore this life will either be blissful or highly unpleasant in some way (the details of this unpleasantness do not matter, at the moment) and it will be God who decides, on the basis of our lives on this earth, which of the two it is to be.

Well it seems to me that these ideas would come across as very odd indeed. To make an obvious point, where is the evidence for this being called God – whom we can never see, or feel, or hear? That is surely what our imaginary non-religious person would immediately ask. If someone of today claimed to believe in fairies or evil spirits, we would immediately demand some evidence for such a bizarre supposition. The same question applies to the amazing properties this God is supposed to possess. It is claimed that he made the universe, out of nothing, simply by some kind of act of will. He is considered to have 'infinite' power, knowledge and goodness – if we can make sense of that. He is a conscious, thinking person like ourselves, who is intimately concerned with every aspect of our thoughts, decisions and behaviour, and who will judge us when we die. Well, again, how can we possibly know all this? Religious believers seldom concern themselves with such a question, obvious though it is. They assume that there must be good reasons, since the doctrines are so widely believed and long-standing. Possibly, if challenged to explain their beliefs, they will refer to the Bible, or some other 'holy book', which they assume – with no real justification – to have some special authority.

There are of course theological arguments for the existence of God, but these are unconvincing (if they were genuine proofs there would be no atheists, as already pointed out) and in any case the vast majority of believers have never seen or thought about these arguments. We have also seen in the previous chapters that there are great difficulties in forming viable concepts of non-bodily entities, and also of finding evidence that any being from some 'other world', some 'higher' order of existence, is causally interacting with this material world. So, at the very least, there is a strong case against religious doctrine in addition to its inherent implausibility.

The question arises, therefore, why religious belief is still so widespread. Belief in wicked spirits, or angels, or 'gods' such as Venus and Mars would now be regarded as superstitions, and perhaps attributed to a need of primitive, pre-scientific people to find explanations. So why does 'God' survive at all, in this scientific age? As said above, I think we will only find the answer by looking at belief itself, rather than the objective case against God.

There is in fact no force more potent than belief in determining the actions of human beings. It is far more influential than, for example, the desire for pleasure, or money, or comfort. Why do some people spend their whole adult lives in monasteries, or convents? Not, surely, for the pleasure this will bring; the regimes required will probably involve considerable austerity and sacrifice. No, they choose the life because they *believe* that that is what God wants from them. Why did Hitler bring about the deaths of millions of Jews? Not – at least primarily – because he was a pathological sadist (if he was that, why attack the Jews, in particular?), but because he *believed* that Jews were harmful to his country. I must stress at once that this in no way justifies him; his actions were evil and wholly to be condemned, of course. But (to modify slightly a well-known dictum of Socrates) very few people do evil willingly, that is while recognising their actions *as* evil. They perform the evil in the mistaken belief that what they are doing is good, or at least justified. The consequences can clearly be tragic in the extreme, as in the case of Hitler and the Jews – but this illustrates the harm that can be done by mistaken belief.

Perhaps a better example of the same kind is that of Mary Tudor, or 'Bloody Mary', who was given this nickname owing to her habit of putting to death (usually by burning at the stake!) Protestants who refused to convert to Catholicism. There has never been any suggestion that she was an evil woman; she was clearly acting out of sincere religious conviction, in the belief that she was carrying out God's will. Thus a false belief resulted in evil deeds which were performed, paradoxically, by a good woman! But innumerable other examples can be given. Suicide bombers provide one of the most extreme and tragic examples. They are willing to give up their own lives in the astonishing conviction that it is desirable and justified to kill or maim other people whose 'offence' is merely to belong to a different nation, or culture, and who are chosen virtually at random. This is one of the most frightening manifestations of the power of belief.

Perhaps the most tragic example of all is provided by war, which is a constant feature of the whole of human history. Consider the suffering that must have been caused in the conflicts of the past, when medical treatment was minimal and no pain-killers existed. And what was achieved? In many cases virtually nothing. The Hundred Years War, with its famous victories at Crécy, Poitiers, Agincourt, was fought to bring France, or large parts of it, under the dominion of England; it was felt, for various arcane reasons concerning rules of

succession, that the English king had a right to the
sovereignty of that country. And yet at the end of the
war, in 1453, virtually all of France was back under the
control of the French. So why was it fought? Largely
because of a completely mistaken (as it now seems to
us) notion of the rights of kings. There were also ideas
about honorable behaviour and the appropriate way to
settle disputes, which are equally alien and incomprehensible to us. These views were held by the *nobility* of
both countries; the ordinary people, who no doubt
endured most of the painful consequences, were
not consulted at all. In fact the suffering, that now
seems such a major factor, seems barely to have been
considered. But once again it is the beliefs, the value
systems of those times, which were responsible. No
doubt the powers-that-be then were no more wicked,
or ill-intentioned, than those of today. But their beliefs
were radically different.

Two final examples of false beliefs resulting in
appalling suffering are the practice of slavery and belief
in witchcraft. The latter was often accompanied with
its (now) incredible accompanying conviction of the
need to burn witches. These practices are so distant
and alien to us that we can easily forget the degree of
pain and injustice involved. That they could happen at
all is surely an indictment of man and his ability to
assess matters fairly and dispassionately. At the risk of
labouring the point, however, it needs to be insisted yet
again that these happenings resulted not (at least
primarily) from any evil intentions on the part of the
perpetrators, but from their mistaken beliefs.

The examples given demonstrate, I hope, that our
systems of beliefs and values – at any rate the fundamental, important ones, those which supply the
principles on which we run our lives – are of enormous

power and influence. It is essential, consequently, that we recognise these beliefs and principles for what they are and examine them carefully. Where they need to be changed, or modified, or scrapped, clearly we should be prepared to do it. But, obvious though this sounds, it is not as straightforward as it may seem. Many beliefs and values are deeply embedded in the mores of our societies. They are taken for granted and often not even correctly identified, let alone questioned or regarded as needing to be questioned. If they happen to be false, therefore, the falsity may never be recognised. And even if falsity is suspected, and a belief is examined, that belief may be difficult or even impossible to over-throw if long-established. Beliefs have a tenacity, a staying-power, which is sometimes quite surprising. But let us begin by considering some of the main sources and causes of false belief, with particular reference to those that bear on belief in God.

Society itself, as just mentioned, is a highly impor-tant source of beliefs and values. We all have many 'background' beliefs, values, principles that we simply take for granted. To appreciate the depth with which these may be embedded, we have only to contrast, say, the mores and principles of a mediaeval village with those of our own. The inhabitants of such a village would accept without question a hierarchical social structure in which the king and noblemen effectively belong to a different order of being from that of the ordinary people. The king would rule by the authority of God; there would be no question of consulting the people over matters of government; such an idea would be considered absurd, monstrous. In such a society women would be seen as 'naturally' inferior to men and therefore subject to men's authority. Probably the religious views would be broadly Christian, but with strong 'superstitious' elements such as belief in spirits and witches.

Now compare this with our own unquestioning belief in democracy, racial equality, equal rights for men and women, the right to healthcare, education and so on.

We now feel quite sure that these latter principles are superior to the earlier ones, and perhaps they are. However, even though these beliefs and principles may in fact be valid, irreproachable, it would a mistake to suppose that the typical person accepts them because *he or she can personally see* that they are rationally grounded. No, we clearly absorb, at least in childhood, the mores of our society without examination, as proceeding from an *authority* that can be trusted. This tendency to accept authority must certainly be something natural, a quality of human beings which is 'hard-wired' into us by evolution. There is no other way for the accumulated knowledge (if it is knowledge) of a society to be quickly and economically transmitted to its new members. Obviously, small children must, as a general rule, accept unquestioningly what they are told by their parents; they have neither the ability nor the means to gain information in any other way. Later this authority is extended to teachers and any other members of society whose position gives them a similar claim.

The key thing to notice is that we habitually, and inevitably, obtain most of our beliefs and knowledge by a reliance on *authority*. This practice is not confined to early beliefs, or ones now seen as superstitions. It applies even to scientific theory, regarded unquestioningly as established fact. If I want to know, say, the distance of the sun from the earth, I can't measure it myself! Nor can I personally test Newton's Laws of

Motion or the principles of electricity and magnetism. I *have* to assume that the books I read, and the teachers who tell me about these things, are true, authentic sources of reliable information. And no doubt that is so in a large majority of cases.

It does mean, however, that if some established belief happens in fact to be false, then *it will be perpetuated by this process just as the true information will.*

It seems impossible to avoid the possibility of error of this kind. And the habit of accepting the teaching of established authority will result in a strong resistance to any attempt to question such teaching.

Let us look a little further at this *permanence* of the values and beliefs we acquire in childhood. It may be objected that I have attributed too much power to the influence of early teaching. After all, although small children necessarily must accept the authority of their parents and teachers, surely older children and adults acquire the ability to think and analyse for themselves, and frequently do come to question the ideas and values of their elders.

Now this certainly does happen up to a point, but I think it is a very limited effect. I would even say that the tendency to retain beliefs is itself a 'hard-wired' feature of human nature. I am talking now of settled, established ideas and doctrines, ones which affect the conduct of our lives, and not, of course, of trivial, passing, day-to-day matters such as the belief that it will rain tomorrow. Again it is easy to see why evolution has built this feature into our nature. Ordinary people – non-philosophers – have to get on with their lives; often very difficult, mundane lives. They have to worry about food, lodging, bringing up their children, perhaps helping to defend their territory from enemies. For this they need principles which are easy to grasp and *reliable;* so by their very nature the principles must have stability, permanence, resistance to change. This need for stable principles was perhaps more obvious in earlier, more primitive times than our own, but it is always true that the majority of people will retain, virtually unquestioningly, the fundamental beliefs, principles and values of their society.

Such permanence, the self-sustaining power of beliefs and values is obvious if we consider actual societies. Let us consider again our earlier example of the inhabitants of an English mediaeval town or village, for example. We have already listed some of their likely unquestioned assumptions.

Now imagine an attempt to introduce, say, some modern liberal principles into such a society. Let us suppose that some mysterious stranger comes along and asks, 'What right has the king to demand your allegiance and obedience?' 'Why do you believe in God?' 'Don't you realise that there is no such thing as a witch?' 'What gives you the right to order your wife around?'

How would the people of that time react to these suggestions? Probably with total bewilderment. One suspects that an ordinary, illiterate peasant would barely understand the questions. A nobleman would probably have the questioner arrested as a dangerous agitator. To achieve an actual change in any of their established beliefs would be virtually impossible.

Now it seems to me that this feature of human nature is still clearly present today. The truth is that human features which have been slowly embedded in us by evolution over countless centuries will be present in mankind's nature permanently, in all circumstances, for better or for worse. Now one of these is that of holding on, tenaciously, to sets of principles and beliefs instilled in childhood. And we cannot decide that now we are an advanced, reflective society, with all sorts of proven means of testing hypotheses, we would be better off to dispose of this tendency to hold on to beliefs. This may indeed be so, but it is not an option. The best we can do is to be aware of the tendency, and allow for its effects. Unfortunately this is easier said than done, and experience shows that few people, even very intelligent, well educated people, succeed in doing it. Giving up a basic, established belief is not 'natural' to us; it is a wrench, which can be painful; and the pain is not necessarily related to the value of the belief; the process operates mechanically, owing to the evolutionary process which has instilled it.

The relevance of the above discussion to belief in God is obvious. The great majority of religious believers are introduced to religious concepts and doctrines in early childhood. They are at that time unable to make any informed judgement as to the strength of the case for these doctrines. The natural processes, instilled by evolution, take effect, and the set of beliefs – whether Christian, Islamic, Buddhist or whatever – may become firmly established. It will not do so for all people, of course; human beings differ greatly in their natural qualities. But for a very large number the doctrines last a lifetime.

The process by which religious doctrines take root and become strongly established is further demonstrated by my second example of how, in a general way, we can acquire false, or at least unjustified beliefs. That is by means of the pressure which can occur, often without our being fully aware of it, through *membership of a group*.

We all belong to groups of various kinds; some large, such as our country or a political party; some much

smaller, such as a school, club, union, employers' asso-
ciation, church, family, set of friends and so on. Now
these groups typically have sets of values. Again these
vary greatly. Some, such as those of a church, are
important and well defined, while others are looser,
perhaps less obvious. But it is likely that membership
of a group will entail some kind of conformity to the
group's values, and, if our membership matters to us,
we can find ourselves under pressure to hold the 'right'
beliefs.

This can be particularly strong for the case of a
church. Suppose, as often occurs, that a person – it
would be typically a young adult – starts to lose confidence in the church's doctrines. Well, the natural
consequence, one might suppose, is to think about
leaving the group – but this could be very painful.
Probably this person has been brought up in the church
and regards it with warmth and affection. His or her
parents belong to it, as do many long-standing friends,
all of whom will be hurt and dismayed if their
companion leaves. So there is strong social pressure to
conform, quite apart from the pain that the loss of faith
itself is likely to involve. And what often happens is that
the person suppresses the doubts; they are pushed
away; he or she thinks about other things – this is quite
easily done. It is in fact rather simpler to do this than
be a conscious hypocrite – to pretend to believe while
knowing that the belief is false. So the belief itself is
shaped, at least to some extent, by the social and group
pressures.

Group pressure can genuinely reinforce and
strengthen belief. It is reassuring to be surrounded by
people who share a common opinion. The belief seems
more likely to be true if it is held by a number of people
whom one likes and respects; conversely it is difficult

to sustain a view that one alone holds: few people have so much confidence in their own judgement. It is also worth mentioning here the power of the 'official' view. That is the position which has become established and is now accepted without question by all the experts. An example is the 'Stratfordian' theory – the belief that the works of Shakespeare were written by the man from Stratford. It is very hard for a single person to stand out against such a position, even if he or she has strong reasons or evidence to doubt the experts. (And often the 'experts' themselves are only relying on the views of earlier 'experts'; a very limited number will have investigated a question independently, with no pre-conceptions.) Now opposing a standard, accepted view can be genuinely dangerous: it can invite ridicule and even threaten a career. It is very easy to become labelled as a 'crank', and lose all chance of being taken seriously. This is certainly true for opposers of the Stratford theory. Thus, again, the power of a 'group' can sometimes perpetuate a false belief.

Another fairly obvious but important influence on our beliefs is *self-interest*. And closely related is the tendency to believe what one *wants* to believe – what one would *like to be true*.

Any honest person will admit to being influenced by self-interest – it is normal and nothing to be ashamed of – a part of human nature. And often we know quite well that self-interest is present and may or may not try to allow for it; this kind of case is unproblematic. What I am interested in now is *hidden* self-interest, that is self-interest which is not evident to the person concerned. A similar, very common occurrence is for someone to believe, and genuinely believe, something that they simply would like to be true. And here I am supposing that the real grounds for the belief are inadequate; the belief actually is caused by the desire, but the believer does not realise this.

It often happens that a belief is held with considerable strength, the believer being quite convinced that it is justified on unimpeachable grounds such as fairness, justice, morality, benefit to the community, or whatever, when its true cause is primarily self-interest. We are not talking about hypocrisy here, a pretence of 'higher' concerns when the person knows quite well that his motives are merely selfish. I am supposing the believer to be genuinely deceived.

A good example of the influence of self-interest is provided by a wages dispute, which, if not resolved, might lead to a damaging strike. Listen to the reasoning of the union leaders and the employers. Both have access to much the same information, but their beliefs about the way the available money should be distributed will be quite different – this is how the dispute arises.

The kind of arguments used are very familiar. The union claims that the firm's prosperity is due to the hard work of its members, and they therefore deserve higher wages; perhaps workers in a similar industry are already paid more. The employers argue that the firm cannot afford these wages. If they are paid the firm's products will have to be priced uncompetitively, jobs will eventually be lost, and so on and so on. Both sides typically have a plausible case: it is rare that one is obviously in the right and the other in the wrong. Usually, in fact, in this kind of case, there is no such thing as the 'right' answer: it is simply up to the two sides to reach an agreement in whatever way they can.

The interesting thing about this kind of situation is the way opinion (and genuine opinion) almost always splits according to self-interest. The union and its members really believe they are entitled to the increase in pay, even to the point of enduring the hardship of a strike. The employers are equally convinced of the merit of their case, and may well fight the strike, even at considerable cost to the profits of the firm. Each side is clearly influenced considerably by self-interest, but does not recognise the fact. This must be so, because if they were genuinely examining the case on its merits, there should be no correlation between, say, being an employer and opposing the wage increase. Genuine impartiality would mean that the split of opinion between employers and union would be in the same proportion as that of a completely impartial, independent panel. But when does this ever occur? If it did happen there would be no dispute.

I realise of course that some strikes are undertaken quite cynically and openly for self-interest. Probably strikes of this kind were quite common in the seventies. But, as already pointed out, this kind of case, where there is no self-deception, is uninteresting. My point is that genuine belief often occurs, which in fact is caused by self-interest, while the believer is quite convinced that he or she is being completely unbiased and fair-minded. This kind of self-deception is very common; it is doubtful whether any of us are entirely free from it.

A closely related source of false belief is simply the *wish* for something to be true. For example, a mother thinks her son or daughter is much brighter than their school realises; it is very rare indeed for the opposite delusion to occur. Or a badly behaved boy is 'really' just high-spirited, or the school is prejudiced against him. A more serious example is that of the relationship between smoking and lung-cancer (along with many other, similar medical cases). When it began to be realised – on good medical evidence – that these were linked, a great many smokers were highly sceptical. A typical reaction would be: 'These doctors, always coming up with some crackpot idea – my uncle smoked 40 cigarettes a day and lived to be 90.' Etc., etc. Clearly the belief here is caused, or at least strongly influenced, by the smoker's *desire* that there should be no link between smoking and cancer. So that a pleasant, entrenched habit need not be painfully broken. This particular way of thinking was only overthrown – in the case of smoking – very slowly and by an accumulation of overwhelming evidence.

I will give just one more example of a source of false belief – or perhaps it would be more accurate to say an influence which tends to *sustain* a belief formed in the past which may be false.

It sometimes happens that a person becomes so convinced about a certain matter that he feels impelled to become a 'crusader' for it. He wants to persuade others; often just friends, but sometimes the whole world. I would put Richard Dawkins in this category, regarding both evolution and the non-existence of God. But the 'crusading' mind-set is very familiar, and it is easy to think of examples. Campaigners for women's rights, members of Shakespeare authorship societies, 'Green' campaigners, religious preachers (particularly the 'fundamentalist' variety) all readily spring to mind. In fact any member of a political party must normally have a pretty strong conviction in favour of its views. By joining the party he or she displays a public personal commitment together with (usually) a determination to try to persuade others. The same could be said of someone who joins a religious order or becomes a religious minister.

The key thing is that a person 'goes public' with his or her beliefs. The commitment is open: the whole world is welcome to know that 'I believe this!' It is such a person that I am now calling a crusader.

Of course this crusading behaviour may be admirable; I don't want to appear to be condemning it in all circumstances. The aims of groups such as political parties and religious orders are after all to benefit others – sometimes at considerable personal cost. (A cynic might dispute this, at least for political parties; but I retain some simple faith!) No, the judgement of the merits of the case is not relevant here; all I am concerned with at the moment is the very strong *reinforcing* effect of becoming a crusader. For such a person the belief is now, in effect, a dogma – something that cannot be questioned. The crusader himself might want to deny that this happens – but can one seriously imagine, say, Richard Dawkins, changing his mind about evolution by natural selection? And it would certainly take a Pauline conversion, a 'Road to Damascus' miracle, to turn Dawkins into a religious believer.

Once one has set out on this path – where one decides to make a case in public, trying to convert others – it is surely impossible, or very nearly so, to jettison one's belief. The 'going public' is a signal that one's mind is made up; the case is clear, proved; there is no longer any point in considering it. And from this time the crusader's energies are no longer directed at the issue itself; that is settled. He is concerned now only with persuading others. Quite apart from the unlikelihood of a genuine change of mind in these circumstances, the blow to personal pride would be a strong deterrent. A loss of status is entailed. After all, if a serious thinker is really certain about something, and then turns out (apparently) to be wrong, what are we to think of his intellectual calibre? No, a change of mind for a crusader is, in the great majority of cases, scarcely practicable.

The situation is fairly similar with a church minister or a member of a political party. They may or may not be active campaigners, but they have made a public commitment – in effect an irrevocable, or near-irrevocable, decision about a set of beliefs. Their whole way of life – certainly in the case of the minister – is determined by that decision, and in most cases a change back, a revocation of the beliefs, is likely to be too radical, too upsetting and painful, to be seriously considered. Such a change is not impossible, and very occasionally it does happen; but the strong reinforcing effect of a public commitment can hardly be denied.

This becomes obvious when a church minister or politician is engaged in a discussion. If a Labour supporter debates some political issue with a Conservative, he doesn't seriously expect to persuade him. (Just try to imagine the Conservative saying, 'Oh yes, there's a good deal in what you say; I'll have to think about this.' A response like that, from a politician, is about as likely as a suspension of the law of gravity!) No, the aim of the discussion is to persuade other listeners, probably a radio or TV audience, hopefully not yet committed. It is much the same if one discusses, say, the existence of God with a religious minister – as I know from personal experience. There is an imbalance in the debate, which makes it rather pointless; one party is (hopefully) open-minded, honestly considering the arguments, while the other already 'knows the truth'. The minister cannot be open-minded; it would be unfair to expect it – in becoming a minister he has made a life-changing decision about the beliefs in question. His object in the discussion is solely to bring the other party from darkness to enlightenment.

The main point I want to make is that becoming a crusader is a big step, and, in a way, a dangerous step, which should be taken with care and hesitation. There probably will be no going back; so one needs to be very sure that one's belief is fixed and justified.

Now how does this discussion bear on the question of belief in God? I would suggest that some and possibly all of the influences described are likely to be operative for the great majority of believers. The effect of upbringing, the influence of parents and society is obvious and has already been looked at. Self-interest and wanting to believe are equally likely to be influential. The fear of death and the instinct to preserve one's own life must make the thought of a blissful, unending existence in 'Heaven' highly attractive. Also there is the idea of God as a 'Father', loving us and wanting the best for us. Then there is the desire for justice, which we have already considered in some depth. It is abhorrent to many to suppose that Hitler and Stalin, for example, should go unpunished, while a morally good person who endures, perhaps, a life of great suffering, should have no compensation, no reward – in fact, be treated at death in just the same way as the great sinners. Again, belonging to groups such as a Christian family, or a Church, will obviously tend to sustain religious belief.

The 'crusading' mind-set, as I have called it, might not be present so often, but it certainly does occur. Priests and ministers clearly have 'gone public' with their beliefs and have made a near-irrevocable decision to base their whole lives on the assumption that God exists and there is a life after death. For them to change their minds must be highly distressing and perhaps humiliating: there is a strong motivation simply to refrain from considering arguments that might threaten their whole way of life. But this applies – admittedly to a somewhat lesser extent – to many ordinary church-goers as well to ministers. We have all met 'militant' believers – not necessarily offensively aggressive people, but ones who make their religious allegiance very clear and seem to regard it as a duty to bring the unbelievers or doubters from darkness into light. These people have made up their minds; they 'know' the truth and are no longer interested in arguments on the other side. Any discussion is purely for the benefit of the unenlightened.

Taking all these considerations into account, I hope I have shown that a widespread belief in God is not difficult to understand, whether or not it is justified. And, to be fair, let us admit that dispensing with God does not remove all the problems which (at least partially) explain the original introduction of the concept of God. In the next, final chapter, we shall look at the case against the main alternative to religious belief, which is materialism. This also presents considerable difficulties. The stance of this book is that the God theory, despite its popularity, in fact fails to stand up to analysis. But this does not mean that we ourselves and our universe are fully explained and understood. Some third theory may be required. Whether we human beings, with our limited capacities, will ever be capable of reaching 'the final truth' must of course be very doubtful.

CHAPTER NINE
ON THE OTHER SIDE

So far we have looked almost entirely at the case against
the existence of God. When this is done it is usually
assumed that the alternative theory – which will be
adopted if the arguments against God stand up – is
materialism. Materialism may be defined as the view
that the physical universe is all there is, or at any rate
all that we are capable of knowing about – so that even
if there are existent things 'outside' it, so to speak, these
things are beyond our reach and therefore effectively
non-existent to us. When I speak of the 'universe' the
reader may wonder if this should actually be seen as
part of a larger entity called a 'multiverse' – a concept
sometimes introduced in popular science programmes.
I do not want to concern myself with this question, By
the universe I include all the material things which are
causally linked to the world we inhabit and thus accessible to us – at least in principle.

The 'God' theory, as we have seen, might be
regarded as an attempt to answer some puzzling questions, such as the origin of this highly complex,
structured and – as some would say – beautiful
universe. Now clearly, if the God theory fails, it does
not mean that these difficult and important questions
disappear. And certainly it is at least disputable
whether materialism provides any better answers. In
this final chapter I want to look at some considerations

that seem to me to tell against materialism. The hope is that we shall end with a balanced position, in which some of the main arguments for and against God and alternative views can be appreciated and their strength fairly assessed. Despite the title of this book, I myself do not want to be seen as strongly anti-God or anti-religion. My final position can probably be best described as one of puzzlement, and perhaps also of doubt whether the human mind can ever adequately grasp these fundamental matters that we are trying to analyse.

Let us begin by looking at 'brute facts'. To remind the reader, these are facts which are basic – they must simply be accepted as true and that is all. The key thing is that these facts *cannot be explained* – for any explanation would have to involve 'prior' facts which would themselves either be explicable or 'brute'. So it seems that brute facts cannot be avoided; they are logically necessary.

Now if we reject God, the natural alternative location for these brute facts must be the universe itself. We could of course try postulating some other 'supernatural' agency to explain the universe, but this would be subject to all the objections that tell against the God theory. For example, how can we possibly know anything about such an entity (or entities)? Could there be any causal interactions between it and this world, and, if so, how could we detect them? Also, as we saw in Chapter 7, the theory of God as creator of the universe does not have the explanatory power it is often credited with. The theory requires highly bizarre brute facts which are at least as difficult to accept as the idea of the universe as brute fact. We have to suppose that a universe (or anything else) will spring into existence whenever the being called God performs some kind of 'act of will'. And there can be no explanation for this – it is just the way things are. Well, clearly any other being with the ability to produce our universe would need the same inexplicable 'power'; so there could be no advantage here over the God theory.

It seems, then, that the 'best' alternative to belief in God is the 'universe as brute fact' view, which was postulated by Bertrand Russell. The problem with this is very simple and may perhaps sound naive. It is that, at least for me, the theory is just highly implausible. It is – again, in my opinion – almost impossible to accept that the physical laws of the universe – those of Newton and Einstein, quantum theory, the laws of electricity and magnetism – operating consistently, over a vast extent of both space and time, are merely inexplicable brute fact. Let us be frank about it, they do seem to suggest *design*. Such a structured universe does look like the result of planning, by a *mind*.

Now it might of course be replied – as suggested above – that this is just a naive reaction. It actually relies on the idea that a brute fact can itself be seen as inherently implausible, and thus *improbable*. But this is surely a fallacy. For probability, or likelihood, can be assigned only on the basis of prior knowledge. A toss of a coin has a probability of a half ('evens', in betting parlance) only on the assumption that the coin is properly constructed with the weight evenly distributed. And the probability that it will rain tomorrow is calculated from a great deal of data about clouds, wind, and so on. Any race-goer or bookmaker will tell you that the odds against a horse winning a race are calculated (or estimated) from a vast body of information including the horse's age and record, the track, the going, the jockey, the trainer, and of course the strength of the opposition. All probabilities, though dealing with the uncertain, are, paradoxically, based on *knowledge* – information of some kind. We cannot obtain the value of a probability from total ignorance.

But, by definition, there can be no prior information about brute facts. So it surely must be a mistake to suppose that any one of these can be more probable than another. We just have to accept them for what they are and realise that explanations are impossible.

This is certainly a plausible argument. Even so, rightly or wrongly, I still cannot feel that it is entirely satisfactory. It seems to me to be impossible to avoid the conviction that some candidates for 'brute' status are simply too strange, bizarre, and thus in some way inherently unlikely, to be accepted as brute facts.

Here is an example. Let us consider the suggestion that the universe actually started five minutes ago. We cannot possibly know this, however, or even have any reason to suspect it, because everything was set up, at this moment five minutes ago, to be exactly the same as we suppose it really was at that moment. All our memories, the archaeological evidence, the books recording the 'facts' about the past, and so on simply sprang into being at that time. The story is obviously designed to make it completely impossible – on the basis of actual evidence – to decide between the normal view of the history of the universe, and this curious alternative suggestion.

Well, it seems to me that on the analysis of brute facts outlined above, there can be no reason to 'prefer' one story to the other. That is because there are no probabilities associated with brute facts. But can we really accept this? If in some way we did discover that the universe started five minutes ago (the practical impossibility of this doesn't matter for the present argument), would we really accept this as just brute fact? Surely such a reproduction of the exact evidence for the orthodox view of the universe would indicate a deliberate attempt to deceive, and thus a *mind* at work. (What sort of mind might cause difficulty – the story probably suggests a malicious demon, a supernatural joker, with more power than judgement!) But whether or not this idea carries conviction, the real point is that some possible 'facts' don't seem to be plausible candidates for 'brute' status, and it is hard to see why this should be so. I do not myself have any answer to this problem, but it just might suggest that the theory of a *designer* of the universe should not be rejected out of hand. The problem with this idea – as outlined in Chapter 7 – lies in the *power* needed for its creation. Such a 'power', as we have seen, itself involves seemingly unlikely brute facts.

This is my first example of a difficulty with the materialist view. To repeat, I do not have the answer to the problem raised: I merely point it out and remind the reader that puzzlement about these matters might turn out to be the only justified final position.

For my next consideration 'on the other side' I am going to look at the curious phenomenon of *consciousness*, and that of the human *person* generally. We are so familiar with conscious persons – for vast numbers of them interact with us all the time – that it is easy to miss the *strangeness* of the entities that we describe as persons.

Let us examine carefully the mind and consciousness. These are very different indeed from inanimate things such as tables and stones; so how are they supposed to have come about in a purely material world – as this earth originally presumably must have been?

Well, that is easy, is it not? They arose, like all properties of living things, by the process of *evolution*. The usual story is that consciousness 'emerges' at some point in the evolutionary process, and this is normally taken to happen at a certain degree of 'complexity' – in the nervous system and particularly the brain. The idea is not limited to materialists; one meets it whenever the phenomenon of consciousness is discussed. 'Complexity', in this context, is typically endowed with extraordinary explanatory power.

But is this really as unproblematic as it sounds? In fact, both of the terms 'emerges' and 'complex' are unclear. 'Emerges', taken literally, seems to imply that consciousness was present before its appearance (presumably in nervous matter) but hidden in some way. If so, we can obviously ask how and where was it hidden and what provoked it to 'emerge'? Perhaps, however, this is an unfair interpretation. Probably all that is meant is that consciousness appears, comes into being, without any suggestion that it already existed. But such an idea is surely very strange. What causes it to appear, brings about its existence? If consciousness is something of a completely different nature from matter – as common sense would suggest – how can merely material processes (chemical reactions or whatever) bring it into being? The only agent ever postulated for this impressive achievement is 'complexity'. But what does this mean?

It seems to me that complexity, at least in this context, can really be nothing more than *plurality*, or multiplicity of ordinary matter; and it is difficult – in fact I would say impossible – to see how this is able to bring into being something so radically new and distinctive as consciousness. This is an utterly different phenomenon from anything we normally associate with matter – with tables and chairs and metal and stone and so on. A computer no doubt has enormously complex circuitry. But this just means that it contains a very great number of circuits (no doubt a staggeringly vast number, but this is irrelevant), each of which in essence is no different from the light circuit in my house. And it is not at all clear how this results in consciousness.

We should not be taken in by the idea of immense complexity; allow ourselves to be awed by huge numbers, so to speak. This is just a relative matter. If we were millions of miles from the earth, examining it through some kind of super telescope, no doubt we should see millions (or billions, for all I know) of electric circuits like the ones in my house, all seeming very tiny, as those of a computer do now. But would there be any temptation to attribute consciousness to these? And if so, where would this consciousness be? At one particular point, or spread over the whole network of circuits? Or is it non-spatial? In fact the consciousness we are familiar with does seem to be connected in some mysterious way with the brain, and move around with it; so the question of locality can hardly be dismissed as meaningless. And of course, to ask the most fundamental and difficult question, which has never been satisfactorily answered in the entire history of philosophy, in what manner is consciousness linked, joined, related, or whatever, to the matter (presumably the brain) which displays this amazing new property?

Here is another approach which might bring home the *strangeness* of persons and consciousness – a strangeness which can easily be missed owing to the familiarity of these phenomena. Look at the *food we eat* – bread, meat, fruit, vegetables and so on. These no doubt are made up of complex molecules; but they are entirely inert – just material things, with no more suggestion of life and consciousness than tables and chairs. But when these substances are taken into our bodies, in some mysterious way (involving DNA, and so on) the cells called *gametes* are constructed – that is cells with all the information needed (when male and female ones are linked) to produce a human being. And such a human being is then constructed out of the very materials – the bread, fruit, and so on; there is nothing else available – which was so lacking in life before entering the body.

And not only is a human *body* produced – that is an immensely complex biological machine which is amazing in its own right – but the entity that we call a *mind* also comes into being at some point, and we have no idea at all how, or exactly when and where, this happens. And this 'something' – mind, soul, ego, or whatever, not only has experiences such as pleasure and pain, but can think, reason, reflect upon moral questions and understand science and mathematics. Furthermore it has *power* to affect the material world around it. For, again in some mysterious way, this 'mind' can determine the motion of 'its' body – principally the hands and feet – and through these means, and in combination with other human beings with similar powers, is eventually able to produce skyscrapers, aeroplanes, complex electrical devices such as TVs, computers and all the rest of the man-made things which inhabit our world. It can also, equally amazingly, perform the actions we call good and evil, and make assessments of what is called *moral value* – something inconceivable for purely material things – in regard to the actions of others. All this is a product – must be a product – of the pieces of bread, meat and fruit which we eat. Every reader is familiar with these happenings; there is nothing here which, for example, is known only by scientists or philosophers. But our familiarity with it masks the strangeness, the deep mystery of consciousness and persons. What is the real nature of these amazing entities we call 'minds', and how do they come into being from such very non-mental material? They seem to be radically distinct, and yet must be somehow linked: we never find minds without bodies, and these bodies both affect and are affected by minds. Furthermore – and perhaps even more striking – we could presumably produce these minds ourselves in a laboratory if we had the appropriate knowledge of chemistry. We could take pieces of bread and meat and from them produce a 'person' who might take decisions which would affect the whole world.

It is important to realise also that there is no obvious reason why consciousness should be limited to brain-matter. Computer experts (who often seem rather to like the idea that computers will eventually take over the world!) frequently speculate on the possibility that computers might at some point become conscious; again 'at a certain degree of complexity'. But this surely adds to the implausibility of the whole 'complexity' thesis. How are we to make sense of this idea that computers 'become conscious'? There is no suggestion that their circuits, however vast in number they become, stop obeying the laws of physics; in fact I have little doubt that the theory of electric circuits studied in sixth form physics is adequate to explain, *in principle*, everything that happens in a computer.

But this means that the processes of a computer are *determined*, fixed by the data put in to it. Of course, we might not in practice be able to calculate what a computer will come up with, purely from our knowledge of the data put in, but this must be completely determined and predictable in theory, as long as the computer obeys the ordinary laws of physics like any other electric circuits. So how could consciousness enter into the matter? What role could it play, and *how would we ever know that it was present?* This is a key question, of fundamental importance. If the laws of physics continue to hold, then everything, on the assumption of consciousness, is exactly as it would be without consciousness. And therefore there could be no possible way to detect it. As I said above, there is no more reason to attribute consciousness to a computer than to my light circuit – or, for that matter, to an armchair or a carpet!

Now this reasoning brings out the real difficulty for the evolutionary theorists who claim that conscious-ness simply 'emerges' during the process of evolution. For the reasoning employed in the case of computers applies just as strongly to the network of brain material which is supposed to display consciousness at a certain stage in evolution. Evolution is a materialist theory, and the whole essence of the theory is that the laws of physics and chemistry alone account for all the mani-festations of life. Evolutionists cannot possibly allow these laws to be suspended, and the laws are predictive, deterministic. So where is the role for consciousness? The paradox is that unless this is given some role in determining the behaviour of matter – behaviour which would necessarily have to differ in some way from what pure physics could bring about – there can be no reason to believe in its existence.

There is yet another difficulty for the materialist approach to consciousness. An essential plank in the evolutionary programme is that developments occur in living things because they are *favourable to survival*. But again, consciousness cannot fill this role if the laws of physics and chemistry alone account for all that happens. How can consciousness be beneficial to survival if it does not have a causal role?

Perhaps the most important point of all, however, is that which was touched on in our discussion of the food we eat. This is that *consciousness is not a purely passive phenomenon*. It is tempting, when we think of complex circuitry, perhaps with electromagnetic waves that interact, possibly produce some kind of 'resonance', and so on, to imagine that somehow or other, when conditions are just right, this produces consciousness rather as an electric current produces a magnetic field. The idea may seem new and surprising, but after all virtually nothing regarding electrical and magnetic fields was known about before the nineteenth century. So perhaps 'the physics of consciousness' is simply something we are only just beginning to be aware of; which, like electricity and magnetism in the early nineteenth century, is yet to be investigated and analysed. We surmise, then, that when the circuitry is just right, sensations like redness, or pain, or pleasure come into being.

This appealing theory, however, is inadequate in one essential, fundamental respect. For sensations are not *self-subsistent* entities which can, so to speak, just hang in the air surrounding the circuits or brain-matter that are supposed to have produced them: they have to be *experienced by something or someone* – this is an essential part of the nature of sensations; it is just the way they are. But what is this 'something' that feels, experiences and presumably thinks, and so on? Well, it must be the entity to which we apply words like 'I', 'ego', 'mind', 'soul' – I am not now advocating any particular word; I don't want to be committed to any ontological theory of the person. But this ego, or whatever we want to call it, is clearly *active*; it makes decisions, and is able somehow to put them into effect. This has to be so, by the reasoning given above; for without such an ability we could have no reason to believe in the existence of consciousness, and, more generally, the mind, at all. This is really quite a surprising conclusion. If the laws of physics still hold, belief in other minds is ruled out by Occam's Razor! Why believe in something which, *ex hypothesi*, is not making the slightest difference to what we can observe?

It is also worth making the more familiar point that, without allowing the ability of a person to make decisions and put them into effect, that is to have an influence on the material world, we should not be justified in praise or blame. There would be no moral qualities, because the world would be governed entirely by the deterministic laws of physics.

The problem of accounting for an *active* ego (or whatever) in conscious beings is particularly striking for the case of computers. Suppose we surmise that, at a certain level of 'complexity', a computer might become conscious. This has to entail some kind of 'ego' (mind, soul, or whatever) which must both have 'experiences' (perhaps sensations, thoughts, speculations and so on), and also 'act' in some way. For, as we have seen, if our conscious entity can make no difference to what happens in the material world, its presence must be undetectable. But this whole idea clearly presents great difficulties for the case of a computer. A *human being* can affect the material world through his or her ability (which is entirely mysterious, as already said) to move the person's own body and thereby other physical objects. But how can our supposed computer 'ego' have a power of this kind?

Setting aside the problem of the location of the ego, what material effects could it possibly produce and what would be the mechanism for doing this? All that seems possible is a modification of the electric currents in the computer and thus, presumably, a suspension of the laws of physics. The motivation for doing this, as well as the thoughts, experiences, feelings of satisfaction, disapproval, and so on – in fact the whole mental 'stream of consciousness' of such an entity, present obvious problems in addition. What could determine the nature of this stream of consciousness, and how could it possibly become known to us, given that the only observable occurrence must be some modification of the computer's electric currents? The more we contemplate this kind of idea (that is, the 'consciousness' of a computer), the more bizarre and mysterious it seems to become.

The conclusion we have now reached is really very strange indeed – it is only our familiarity with minds and mental phenomena that masks this strangeness. Our story is as follows. Millions (or billions) of years ago, this earth consisted entirely of inanimate matter, governed solely by the laws of physics and chemistry. By chance a self-replicating molecule arose, and, still by ordinary chemical interaction and so on, through the operation of purely mechanistic laws, entities that we call organisms (amoebas, perhaps primitive fish, and so on) evolved. And these were still no more, in their essential nature, than very complex and intricate machines; in effect super-robots, whose entire behaviour continued to be governed by ordinary physics and chemistry.

Then, at an unknown point in the evolutionary process, something *apparently* of a quite different nature appeared – what we call broadly the mind and mental phenomena. Now minds seem to have their own causal properties, which operate on matter and somehow differ in the effects they have from mere physical laws. For, by the arguments given above, it is hard to see how we could have any reason to believe in the presence of mind if this were not so. But how can this be? Where did these strange entities come from and how can they possibly interfere with, or even override, the physical laws? Surely they must be part of the natural world, and therefore subject to its laws. So do our ordinary physical laws provide an incomplete account of the world, or do minds somehow operate within those laws? Or are we forced to be really radical and postulate that mental entities differ in their fundamental nature from the stuff of the material world? Could they, for example, belong to a 'higher', spiritual realm?

The last suggestion would no doubt be welcomed by people of religious bent; it would certainly be rejected with scorn by materialists. For myself, I simply want to claim that the arguments point to a problem which at present has not been solved. The origin of the mind, and mental qualities generally, is not yet properly understood. I should make it clear that I am not going to rush back to God, as it were, to provide a solution – it is too easy to fill gaps in our knowledge by invoking God. So I do not, for example, believe that God, at a certain point in the development of every embryo, injects a little supernatural soul into its brain by a sort of spiritual pipette! (This is one extreme version of the 'dualist' theory of mind and body.) In criticising materialism I am not claiming that there is an easy solution to the problem of the mind – if we only invoke God, for example. My objection is that materialists typically fail to realise that the mind and consciousness present any problem at all – and the problem is in fact particularly damaging to their theory.

The key point to grasp is that if the movements of our bodies are determined by purely physical laws, then, to put it bluntly, we are just super-robots. We are completely deluded when we suppose that we are making free decisions as to how our bodies move. Certainly, if this is so, there can be no justification for praise and blame. And, as pointed out already, it is hard to see, on evolutionary grounds, why the mind should have made an appearance at all, since it has no real influence on what happens. I think this theory is too paradoxical, indeed too incredible in every way, to be seriously considered.

For my final example of the apparent inadequacy of materialism I am going to look at the so-called 'moral law'. This brings in concepts such as good, evil, right, wrong, ought, duty and so on – concepts very familiar to human beings but which are hard to explain on a materialist basis.

The question is how to analyse these concepts – this is in fact one of the oldest problems in the history of philosophy, and it has never been solved satisfactorily. When I decide it is a 'good thing' to help some person who is in trouble, or I describe, say, a rape or a murder as 'wrong', or 'evil', what exactly am I saying? What is the nature of these mysterious qualities? They are not like 'six feet tall', or 'made of iron' or 'green'. The latter properties (which are called 'empirical') are detectable by our senses or investigable by science, and are relatively unproblematic. But no sense can detect 'goodness'. And if two people disagree about whether a particular action is morally good, there is no easy way to settle the matter. We can't say, 'look more carefully', or 'do this experiment', or something of the kind. So the nature of moral qualities, if they exist at all, presents a problem.

This problem is too complex and difficult to be analysed in depth at the moment. But fortunately all we need concern ourselves with now is whether any kind of *reductionist* theory might work, or at least be plausible. That is, a theory which reduces the concepts to something more familiar – and takes away any need to treat them as mysterious, *sui-generis*, in other words qualities which cannot be accommodated in a materialist theory of the universe. If it turns out that moral qualities cannot be explained in this way, it is further evidence of the inadequacy of materialism.

One plausible attempt to explain moral qualities is to link them to the production of human *happiness*. (Or perhaps *welfare* is a broader and more satisfactory term.) Theories of this kind are known as *utilitarian*. There are many variations, but the essential idea is what we now call the moral law is really a distillation of principles of behaviour which have been found, over a long period of time, to maximise human happiness or welfare. Thus the morally *right* action, in a given situation is that which achieves this or can be reasonably expected to do so. There are obvious difficulties, of course, one of which is simply that of how to measure human happiness, as well as misery and pain. There are no *units* of happiness or pain!

A more profound problem, however, is that maximising happiness may involve a violation of human rights. (It may of course be claimed that there is no such thing as a 'human right', but most people would not agree.) An amusing story which illustrates this point is to suppose that there are three people in hospital, one of whom needs a heart transplant and one a new kidney. They will die if these organs cannot be found. The third patient has an ingrowing toenail, but a perfect heart and kidney. We can make the story more striking by supposing that the first two are of enormous value to the community (a Newton and a Beethoven perhaps) while the third is a worthless layabout. Now utilitarianism would surely say that we should kill the layabout and use his organs to save the other two (assuming that the technology is reliable and the operations are virtually certain to succeed). This would almost certainly lead to more human happiness, or welfare, than letting them die. All our moral instincts, however, rebel very strongly against the idea. The layabout surely has a *right* not to be killed.

Of course this does raise the question of how much reliance can be placed on moral intuitions. Can we trust these? Are we perhaps deluded and really should be strictly logical and kill the layabout?! (This is the 'tough-minded' utilitarian approach.) It could be, after all, that evolution has implanted these moral 'intuitions' and they have no real validity. Another view is that they are some kind of perceptions of objective truth. I am afraid there is no definitive answer to this kind of question, but – for what it is worth – I myself incline to the latter view.

In any case, however, it seems to me that all theories of this kind fail to do justice to the concepts of good, evil and so on that we actually hold. If moral principles are really only ways of maximising happiness, then happiness is being regarded as the supreme good for mankind – that which takes precedence over all else. But suppose I don't accept this – or I am so constituted that the welfare of humanity has no importance for me. Then there is no reason why I should obey the ordinary moral rules. It is just a matter of choice; there is no compulsion in the matter, no *law* which has to be obeyed. There is nothing *absolute* in moral values, for me.

That, however, is not at all the way moral laws are actually seen by the great majority of mankind. There is one characteristic of moral judgements which is generally accepted – they *override all other considerations*. To illustrate this, suppose I have a choice between action A and action B. Action A wins me a large sum of money, but it is generally agreed that it would be morally wrong to perform this action and that action B is the morally right course. Well that 'rightness' settles the matter; debate is at an end. It is unquestionable that I ought, I have a moral *duty*, to perform B. This conviction of the presence of duty, of a *law*, cannot be accommodated by theories which base morality on human welfare.

The conclusion just reached, which is very important, can perhaps be demonstrated more strongly by comparing moral and *aesthetic* judgements. Both of course are examples of *value judgements*, and superficially not dissimilar. The difference however is critical, and I think that contrasting the two cases brings out the particular character of moral qualities which is relevant here.

Consider a great picture, painted by a famous artist. How should we describe such an object? Well, it will have a size and shape, be constructed with paint of various colours, arranged in patterns which might be described geometrically, and so on. These are the normal *physical* qualities which are discernible by observation. But these do not account for the *value* we place on the picture. To explain this value we need to say that the picture has a quality such as *beauty* (the principal *aesthetic* quality) in addition to its physical character. Now clearly beauty (together with other aesthetic qualities) is a property of a very different kind from the physical attributes, even though grammatically this might not be obvious. The description, 'The painting is four feet tall', is superficially similar to, say, 'The painting is beautiful'. But there are plenty of properties that sound grammatically like 'four feet tall', and are clearly very different in their true natures. Examples might be, 'admired by John'; '100 miles from Manchester'; 'worth 20 million pounds'; 'painted 500 years ago'. None of these are *intrinsic* qualities, which the painting has *in itself*; they simply describe ways in which it is related to other things.

What, then, are we to say of beauty? It is hard to believe that in addition to all the physical qualities there is *also* some mysterious property called beauty; how could this 'attach itself', so to speak, to the object? What would we say of a landscape that would be called beautiful if seen, but which in fact no one has ever seen? Does it have beauty, though no one has ever experienced this? Does it have anything at all (in its true, intrinsic nature) other than its physical properties? Surely not. If it does 'really' have beauty, well this beauty must be a very odd and puzzling property – certainly non-physical, for no scientific instrument could detect it. We might almost call it a mystical property.

No doubt some people do believe that in some peculiar way beauty and other aesthetic qualities really belong to objects. But it not *necessary* to postulate this. And on the principle that we should not introduce supposedly existent things without good reason ('Occam's Razor') it is not *justified* to believe in the objectivity of beauty. There is in fact a simple, non-mystical analysis which seems to me to be perfectly adequate for this kind of case. Surely beauty is nothing other than a *causal* property; it refers to the *effect* the picture has on viewers who, through natural ability, or the effect of training, are capable of responding aesthetically to it. (This effect, which is virtually impossible to describe, can be profoundly moving, of course.) Admittedly there can be problems as to when it is justified to describe some particular thing as beautiful. How many people have to get the proper response? Should we consider only the 'consensus of expert opinion', when deciding whether something is truly beautiful? These are matters for the theory of aesthetics (another branch of philosophy), and they are not relevant to the present discussion. The important thing to see is that beauty resides in a beautiful object only in the form of a *power to produce a reaction or effect.* So we do not need to postulate anything mysterious, non-natural, to account for aesthetic qualities. We can retain a materialist view of the world.

Now it is possible to put forward a similar (reductivist) theory of moral concepts, judgements and behaviour. This analysis runs somewhat as follows. When confronted with a moral situation we (if we are normal human beings) have an *experience of approval or disapproval,* and perhaps an impulsion to act in a certain way. This has come about, of course, because such a response is evolutionarily favourable: it promotes the survival and welfare of the human race.

The moral experience (according to this theory) is of a particular, distinctive kind, like the aesthetic experience. It is roughly describable as 'approval', or 'disapproval', but it needs to be realised that moral approval has its own character which distinguishes it from other sorts of approval. We might approve of a cricket shot, or a particular way of gardening; but this is very different from the *moral* experience we get when, for example, we think about a person who 'lays down his life for his friend'. Equally, there may be non-moral disapproval. A carpenter, say, might experience this on seeing a bungling DIY enthusiast trying to construct a chair. Or a concert pianist could feel (very painful) non-moral disapproval on hearing an amateur bang out a popular tune. These experiences are entirely different from the distinctive *moral* outrage which rape or murder might induce in us. But the key point is that, according to the Darwinian analysis, these reactions are a consequence of our genes, which, by purely physical means, have developed the power to induce such responses in us. This has happened because the responses, directly or indirectly, are favourable to the gene's survival.

It will be seen that the above account is similar, in essentials, to the analysis of beauty as a causal property. This does not require any notion of beauty as an intrinsic property, and, similarly, the Darwinian analysis of morality does not require us to suppose that moral qualities *really* belong to human actions. The theory is not new; it was formulated, without the Darwinian accompaniments, by David Hume in the eighteenth century. In a well-known passage from the *Treatise on Human Nature*, Hume says:

> Take any action allowed to be vicious, wilful murder, for instance. Examine it in all lights, and see if you can find that matter of fact, or real existence, which you call vice. In whichever way you take it, you find only certain passions, motives, volitions, and thoughts. There is no other matter of fact in the case. The vice entirely escapes you, as long as you consider the object. You never can find it, till you turn your reflection into your own

breast, and find a sentiment of disapprobation, which arises in you, towards this action.

It can be seen that this is a *subjectivist* theory of morality, like the account of beauty above. Hume's view is that there is no real moral quality in an action itself, but that the morality consists *solely* in the feeling of approval or disapproval which it tends to produce in normal human beings. He also claims, plausibly enough, that we are so constituted that the happiness or misery of others tends to excite *sympathetic* pleasure or pain in ourselves. This means that the experience of approval tends to be directed towards activities which promote happiness and disapproval towards those which tend to produce pain. Consequently conventional morality tends to lead towards a net increase in human happiness. Hume's theory is thus superficially similar to that of the utilitarians, though with a very different rationale.

Let us now try to see why the subjectivist analysis of morality does not work, while that of beauty does. The two cases are in fact radically different, and to see this we need only to examine this feeling of approval, and contrast it with the experience of beauty. The key point is that approval, by its very nature, is approval *of* something other than itself; it seems to have the character of a *judgement* about how things actually are – which is very different from a private, internal occurrence like an experience of beauty or a sensation such as the taste of strawberries. In the case of the experience of beauty, or the taste of strawberries, the value, the reason for our enjoyment, lies entirely in the sensation or experience itself. But in the case of approval, *the value lies in the thing approved*; the internal feeling has no value in itself. In fact, if the feeling of approval exists in the absence of something worthy of that approval, the feeling, which is essentially a judgement, is delusory, and we would be better off without it.

Notice the radical difference here between morality and aesthetic experience. If I dislike a famous Mozart symphony – it fails to give me the aesthetic response others enjoy – no *obligation* follows; there is no 'ought' in the matter. I might *choose* to try to 'educate my taste', and learn to appreciate the music as others do; but if I choose not to, that is a matter for myself alone: mine is the loss, if there is any loss. Similarly I might choose or not choose to learn to appreciate a fine wine: it's up to me entirely. But if I see a small child drowning, and I can swim, it is not 'up to me' whether I try to save him. I can't say, 'Sorry, it's inconvenient; I'm in a hurry, and I don't want to get wet.' The two cases are totally different – different in their essential natures. But on the Hume analysis they should not differ at all.

Here is another way to look at the matter. Suppose that we could take a drug which would induce us to experience a taste of strawberries when we have to take some unpleasant medicine. Clearly this would be an excellent thing; it is perhaps a pity that (as far as I know) such drugs do not exist. But now suppose we could take a drug which would make us experience a feeling of moral approval on witnessing, say, a murder. Would this make the murder *really* morally better? Well, the idea is clearly absurd; we might as well imagine a drug which makes us believe that $2 + 2 = 5$. But on the subjectivist analysis it should not be absurd, because true moral value lies solely in the feelings it induces. This argument alone, it seems to me, shows the inadequacy of the subjectivist theory of morality.

The two final problems with materialism that we have identified, that of the origin of the mind and the problem of morality, are actually complementary. They both concern the existence and properties of *persons, human beings*. It is here that the real difficulty for materialism lies – simply in *ourselves*, in the fact that we exist at all. For the moral law can only apply to a *person*, which is an entity of an entirely different nature to purely material things. As long as there are no minds, no consciousness, there can be no moral law. That is obvious. A person, with free will, is required before we can talk of morality. Now we saw, earlier in this chapter, that the standard, mechanistic account of evolution cannot explain the appearance of conscious-ness, minds and thus persons: we now see, approaching the problem from a different direction, so to speak, that the theory cannot account for morality. That is of course unsurprising, given the linked nature of the two problems. The conclusion of both approaches, along with the difficulties we found with the 'brute fact' theory of the universe, must be that there is something fundamentally unsatisfactory and inadequate about materialist theories.

What, then, is the final conclusion of the book? We said at the beginning that agnosticism might ultimately be impossible to avoid, but that this should be adopted only after a proper investigation, and not result merely from an inclination to 'give up the struggle'. I think that we are now in a position to say that neither of the two standard theories (God and materialism) can satisfac-torily deal with all the problems which are thrown up by the existence of our universe, and of ourselves, and that therefore agnosticism is justified. The God theory might be seen, charitably, as an attempt to solve our problems which in fact fails but which can be under-stood and regarded sympathetically.

INDEX